"STORY" IN POLITICS

"STORY" IN POLITICS

MICHAEL NOVAK

COMMENTARY BY

TRAN VAN DINH
DAVID LITTLE
DANIEL C. MAGUIRE
THEODORE R. WEBER

Michael Novak is Provost of the Disciplines College, State University of New York at Old Westbury. His writings include *Belief and Unbelief, A Time to Build,* and most recently, *A Theology for Radical Politics* and *The Experience of Nothingness.*

Tran Van Dinh, now a writer and lecturer, was in the South Vietnamese diplomatic service and last served as chargé d'affaires in Washington in 1963. A member of the South Vietnamese Cabinet in 1960, he held the portfolio of Director-General of Information.

David Little is Assistant Professor of Christian Ethics in the Divinity School of Yale University, where he is a specialist in historical and social ethics. He is the author of *American Foreign Policy and Moral Rhetoric,* published by CRIA.

Daniel C. Maguire, Associate Professor of Christian Ethics at The Catholic University of America, has been a frequent contributor to CRIA publications and other programs.

Theodore R. Weber is Associate Professor of Social Ethics at Candler School of Theology, Emory University, and a frequent contributor to scholarly and religious journals.

Copyright 1970 by

THE COUNCIL ON RELIGION AND INTERNATIONAL AFFAIRS

170 East 64th Street, New York, N. Y. 10021

All rights reserved

Printed in the United States of America

Library of Congress No. 73-150866

JX
1417
.N67

FOREWORD

It is not inevitable that the ongoing political debates in this country will engage the fundamental issues of United States foreign policy. But they should. Even among those who disagree most strenuously about what our foreign policy has, in fact, been over the last several decades, and what it continues to be today, there is general agreement that we must forge new policies for the coming decades.

But on what basis should those new policies be based? What are the principles or guidelines that will improve the practice of United States foreign policies? Will new policies be based primarily on the evidence that the world has changed since the middle 1940's when our present policies were developed and the subsequent conviction that our policies must change accordingly? Or can we achieve additional or new or improved methods of considering and developing foreign policy? Will these new methods, if they exist, allow us to discern more clearly those moral issues that have been propelled, sometimes violently, into our present political discussions?

In an attempt to address himself to some of these questions and their implications, Michael Novak has invoked the category "story." It is his intention, by employing this category, to analyze and illumine both political theory and practical politics. And it is the intention of those who comment on his

227429

essay to evaluate the merits of his proposal and of his accomplishment. It is a collective hope that, interjected into our present debate, this exchange will clarify what is obscure, deepen what is shallow, and advance what is new.

A word should be said about the genesis of this publication. In 1968, CRIA initiated a study group, i.e., it brought together a number of scholars and writers who agreed to meet and explore at regular intervals some aspects of "religion and international affairs." Michael Novak prepared for one of these sessions the essay published here. The commentaries are intended to reflect some of the discussion provoked by that essay. Since Tran Van Dinh did not participate in the sessions of the study group his contribution, presented for its intrinsic merit, is the single exception to this pattern.

James Finn
Director of Publications

Council on Religion and
International Affairs

Contents

"STORY" IN POLITICS

Michael Novak

The category "story" illumines certain realities of practical politics and clarifies certain issues in political theory. "What role should nation X play in theatre of operations Y?" "What role should person Z play in the government?" We frequently use such metaphors in seeking to define the course of political action. But no systematic attention has been paid to typing, cataloguing, and analyzing the finite number of political stories which seem, so far, to be operative in the political history of the United States, or in the larger field of international politics today. I would like to shed some light on the category "story," and to exploit some of its potency in an analysis of certain arguments concerning the American involvement in Vietnam.

Many arguments in the field of international politics, in particular, go astray because of a failure to distinguish several logical levels of political argument. It would be easier for all of us if speech about politics did not move on so many levels at once. But many matters are at stake in international politics.

I. A BRIEF ANTICIPATION

International politics is, in the first place, an arena of constant change and constant interaction. It is the arena of human freedom and human determination: man is the only animal whose future is not determined solely by biology and environmental accident. But the arena of change and human determination has a temporal dimension; events occur in it over time. And human agents—individuals and collectives—act in time. Consequently, all political thinking is, in one way or another, narrative thinking. Every nation, every alliance, every national leader or party has a story: and not only a story as the record of a past, but a story as the projection of a future.

One story about the United States, for example, includes the discovery of "a new world," marvellously rich and awesome: a kind of paradise, a place for a "new beginning" for the human race. A nation slowly takes shape in the new land and, in due time, is "born." On its currency, the dollar bill, is imprinted the fundamental motif: *novus ordo seclorum,* "the new order of the ages." Wandering in a kind of innocence in seemingly virgin wildernesses, the American imagines himself a "new Adam," starting anew, without the entanglements, corruption, and evils of the history of the European peoples he left behind. The new nation is launched with a creed, the "Declaration of Independence," expressing implicitly a faith in reason, in God, and in human universality—as if, to match a virgin and rich continent, man had attained a level of enlightenment which at long last promised a new justice, a new equality, a new freedom as possibilities for the new land and, ultimately, for the world. New land and new ideals were wed. The American story is aspiration toward a new international order: a nation pledged to "liberty and justice for all" its own citizens, and not only that, but in consistency (for its understanding both of God and of reason committed it to the universality of its fundamental values), pledged also to the support of liberty and justice elsewhere in the world.

If liberty, justice, and equality define a type of human moral goodness, then Americans are publicly committed to being a good people among world peoples—to teaching by example, to being an example. The American story is, in this version, a story of the pursuit of national goodness, a goodness to be made manifest also in international affairs. Americans do not start wars for ignoble purposes (i.e., contrary to ideals of liberty, justice, equality); do not conduct wars in ignoble ways (as a matter of calculation and deliberate policy); do not enter wars eagerly or even willingly.

The innocence of America's origins was not entirely naive; the birth of the Republic required the travail of a five-year revolutionary war because of the obstinateness of the corrupt institutions of the old order (the British Crown). White Americans maintained the story of innocence even through their protracted wars to eliminate the "savages," whose land their power enabled them simply to claim as their own. The story of innocence was also maintained despite the dependence of the Southern economy on slavery. The bitterness of the Civil War, however, the most destructive war in human history until that point, introduced a further moral maturity into the original story of innocence: Americans in an innocent land could kill one another. A brave and good man, Abraham Lincoln, rescued the story of innocence by deepening it with the motif of reconciliation: emancipation of the slaves, malice toward no American, union preserved.

The idealism of Woodrow Wilson during the first world war, the revulsion against foreign entanglements which led to the isolationism of the 1930's, the enormous outburst of national energy for the "Crusade in Europe" and in the Pacific Theatre in World War II, and the resolute determination since 1948 to "contain communism" add new motifs and modifications to the fundamental story. America has never been forced to imagine itself as a fundamentally corrupt, self-interested, tyrannical nation in world affairs. Despite her immense power and far-flung military presence, the fundamental story, in this version, has remained unchanged: successive chapters in the journey toward equality, liberty, and justice for all men.

What is new at the present moment in the history of the United States is that a growing number of Americans no longer believe this American story; and that a growing number of persons in other nations—who, for the most part, often did accept the story of America in roughly the American way—also have ceased to believe it.

To be sure, the "realists" in the American tradition, those who, as David Little puts it, belong to the "tradition of liberal disillusionment," seem to have embraced the maxim: *Moralism and idealism in international affairs produce more harm than good.*[1] They tried to introduce a sense of complexity, immorality and ideological blindness into the political consciousness of America. They tried to persuade Americans to be less pious (Reinhold Niebuhr), less innocent (Graham Greene), less arrogant (Senator Fulbright), less given to moral abstractions (Hans Morgenthau), less idealistic (Robert F. Osgood), less legalistic-moralistic (George Kennan), etc. David Little himself objects to the ideological blinders

[1] *American Foreign Policy and Moral Rhetoric* (New York, 1969), pp. 8, 14, *passim.*

present in the maxim stated above. He rewords it: "In *some* foreign policy situations moral rhetoric can be used to cloak devious motives and self-seeking objectives."[2]

In a word, events in recent decades have led prominent American thinkers to have doubts about the legacy of American foreign policy. They question both the fundamental story and the new doctrinaire attacks upon that story. The war in Vietnam, it cannot be forgotten, has been primarily a realists' war;[3] few criticisms of it were forthcoming from realists until very recent years. It was not a war enthusiastically entered into by the traditional parties of moralism; it was from the beginning calculated in terms of limited interests. It is a war that has plunged the realists into disarray. It has done so because the realist tradition did not modify American political consciousness on a sufficiently deep level.

Realism tried to dispel moralism and to promote a closer calculation of real interests. But its vocabulary for discussing interests was too impoverished. Its expectations were not sufficiently sensitive to understand the situation in Vietnam. Its grasp of "reality" was too limited. I would like to propose the use of a language for international affairs that allows for a somewhat fuller discussion of differences in consciousness and hence in views of reality. We require a methodological shift the equal of that achieved by William James, Pierce, Dewey and dozens of others who, by 1910, had codified the "pragmatism" by which we have lived these last fifty years.

[2] *Ibid.*

[3] William Pfaff, "The Liberals' War," *Commonweal* (September 15, 1967), pp. 350-51. See also Richard H. Rovere, *Waist Deep in the Big Muddy* (Boston, 1968).

II. THE INTERPRETIVE RICHNESS OF POLITICAL ACTION

Men and nations are finite: they cannot act from an infinite number of points of view, nor play all roles in all stories at once. Action requires a focusing of attention and effort; it requires selection from among possibilities. For action is concrete, finite, determinate; it narrows down the fuzzy area of vagueness, drift and inactivity; it involves one in definitions. Choices limit the future, and thus sometimes it is wise not to act, or not to act too decisively. Still, the limitations placed upon the future by choice are, in the long run, necessary conditions of effectiveness. If choices do not define the future, the future will, nevertheless, be defined.

To discuss action intelligently, however, one must be aware of many different levels of discourse. Human experience is extraordinarily diffuse and amenable to an almost endless variety of shapes. Preparing to act, we ask our advisors such questions as: What's up? What are the facts? What's our long-range strategy? What should I do first? How should I disguise my intentions? What roles will my associate play? Do I need to maneuver to get the action to a specific arena? At what point do I irrevocably commit myself? What can I do to make others commit themselves first? The category story includes these and similar questions.

The tendency in Anglo-American discussions of political and ethical action is to examine such questions under three categories, with the recent addition of a fourth. Theoretical discussions center on ascertaining: (1) the facts; (2) the principles (imperatives, policies, goals); and (3) the options (sequences of means)—but the practical, immediate selection of means is most often left to the agent in the field. Recently, because of the impressive role of television and mass communications, increasing attention is paid to (4) image projection.

Such emphases tend to carry with them faint memories of rationalist philosophers making moral proposals. More exactly, the model of rationality seems to be that of engineers planning how to dispose of *X* resources in situation *Y* for purposes *Z;* public relations enter as an afterthought. The underlying model for policy discussions appears to be that of a problem in business administration. Not only do the explicit metaphors often used in policy discussions—cash value, costs, cost-effective, efficient, hard sell, soft sell, build-up, backlog, reserves, personnel—convey the mood and expectations of the business world. It is also the case that the whole point of view, even if such metaphors as those mentioned were scrupulously avoided, seems to envisage human action as a species of economic transactions: one organizes for international politics as one organizes for producing and selling a new product.

Thus, for example, the situation in Vietnam during 1961-1965 seems to have been examined by assessing: (1) the relative resources in men and material of "enemy" and government forces; (2) the principles of "resist aggression" and "defend allies" ("self-determination" and "freedom" always had in Vietnam a slightly more hollow ring); and (3) a series of options which could only be escalatory in nature since, in the calculation of resources, the initiative lay always with the enemy. The importance of (4) public relations had been well attended to in the selling of Diem to the American media, and in the steady flow of optimism from Saigon.

But what the Vietnamese have been teaching Americans—the "government Vietnamese" by their uncharacteristic childlikeness and passivity in war, the "enemy" by their actions—is that the American realist's sense of reality does not coincide with the sense of reality practiced by other people in other cultures. What American realists think not worth dying for other people will die for. What American realists think superstitious will seem to some others most real. Quantification, which is most real to American realists, will seem fanciful to them. The psychology of the Viet Cong guerrilla is not that of the American soldier. Their senses of reality diverge; their estimates of events, emotions, facts, actions and sequences of actions diverge. Similar frustrations arise between American advisors and South Vietnamese advisees. The point about these frustrations is that they are almost total: experiences, images, understandings, judgments and values diverge. The fundamental project is understood in fundamentally divergent ways.

III. THE LOGIC OF POLITICAL ACTION

A better schema for dealing with the many levels of discourse about action would go, I believe, something like this. A single action (or report of an action) takes its meaning from the principle (or interpretive schema) that informs it. A principle takes its meaning from the concrete symbol that informs it. A story takes its meaning from the sense of reality that informs it. Hence, we have the sequence of levels of meaning:

sense of reality→story→symbol→principle→act or event

One cannot define the meanings at the lower end of the scale without understanding the meanings at the higher end. The meanings at the higher end supply the criteria and the expectations by which the meanings at the lower end are defined.

My thesis is that American political thinking pays for too little explicit attention to sense of reality, story, and symbol, and hence characteristically misperceives the bearing of international actions. American theoreticians (and practical politicians) are much too confident about the universal validity of their own sense of reality. They are not sufficiently aware of the grip their own historical stories exercise over their imagination, nor sufficiently sensitive to critical differences in stories not their own. Finally, they confound their own principles—liberty, equality, justice—with the concrete symbolic forms by which these principles are understood and institutionalized in the United States. It may not seem sufficiently "rational" to American theoreticians to treat—explicitly and with discrimination—senses of reality, stories, and symbols when analyzing, for example, the situation in Vietnam. Impatience may arise; for what do sense of reality, story, and symbol have to say to the *real* issues? The American sense of reality systematically downgrades attention to sense of reality, story, symbol. For it is precisely the American sense of reality to understand "rational," "reasonable," and "real" in terms of the principles and facts at the lower end of our scale of meanings.

In order to proceed clearly, therefore, I advance the following stipulative definitions. (It will not suffice merely to cite dictionary meanings of sense of reality [myth], story, or symbol. In the first place, American usage is systematically biased. The words myth, story, and symbol are used in opposition to the "true," "factual," "verified"; the fundamental questions are thereby begged. For what if the American bias in favor of principle and fact is not a sufficient guide to what is true, factual, verifiable? Apart from the empirical sense of reality, the story of clear definitions and hard facts, and the symbols of distinctness and hardness, how would one know what is to count as fact? Secondly, such large epistemological questions are involved that economy of discussion seems better served by stipulation than by philosophical argument. Still, the latter is clearly called for; I hope to meet it soon in book form.)

Definitions

1. A *report* is a description of an event or an act. "I kept my promise." (A *sequence* of acts or events is described by a *story*.)

2. A *principle* is a prescription, the definition of a goal, a policy, or the conceived object of an attitude. It does not give the motive, intensity, or style to action; it gives action its conceptual and abstract form. "Keep promises." "I want my word to be trusted." "Our first policy decision is to keep those pledges we have made." "Promise-keeping: hurrah!"

3. A *symbol* is a concrete image which triggers emotion and catalyzes action. Symbols give action their motive, intensity, and style. The cool, dispassionate investigator; disrespect by others towards the flag; the word "Communist"; tenure at Harvard.

4. A *story* is an imagined form linking actions in ordered sequences: "The Communists invaded South Vietnam and have been attempting to undermine an independent govern-

ment whose sovereignty has been recognized by over sixty nations."

Stories function in three ways. They provide the sequential form in which to situate past actions, in which to specify the context and meaning of present actions, and by which to shape future actions. In its first function, "story" is like "report" (except that "report" applies to a single event or act, whereas "story" involves a sequence of events and acts). The second and third functions establish the basic meaning of "story" as a political category: to give meaning to the present and guidance for the future.

A story links symbols. A story expresses the form of action and the temporal dimension of a sense of reality. *Principles* (policies) state the conceptual, cognitive, abstract intelligibility of action; they state the essentials clearly and sharply. For that reason, principles often have a liberating, critical effect upon the concrete frame of reference composed by symbols and stories (local customs, traditions, prejudices, myths). On the other hand, principles by their very abstractness are coercive and disruptive of the concrete tissue of life. The Protestant story (a theology of the Word), favoring clarity and universal principles and demythologization, smoothes the way for the universal pretensions of modernization, urbanization, and bourgeois democracy. In any case, action is not thoroughly understood until both its concrete density and its conceptual intelligibility have been discerned. A story is to a principle (policy) as existence to essence. A college president who enunciates liberal principles may act in an arbitrary, authoritarian, managerial style; a man of authoritarian principles may, in the concrete, act openly, fairly, wisely. A man's story gives concrete shape to his principles. Political theory needs to be as explicit and careful in diagnosing his story as in analyzing his principles. (Lyndon Johnson as liberal.)

5. Myth is a word usually used of other people's *sense of reality.* A myth is, in fact, a sense of reality. It is a cultural (or personal) shaping of experience, imagination, understanding, judgment, and decision. To discover your own myth, examine what you consider realistic.

What I intend by the category "sense of reality" is, because it is prior to conceptual definitions, difficult to make clear. Each man's sense of reality is so close to him, so much a part of his memories, perceptions, and anticipations, that he seldom becomes aware of it. Usually, one notices its contours best in another country under conditions of "cultural shock," when one's own frame of reference seems either to fail or to falsify: when arguments do not make sense, when perceptions are confused, when fundamental criteria are diverse. Under such conditions, the lower levels on the scale outlined above are each thrown out of focus. When one's sense of reality fails, one's stories, symbols, principles and facts are without mooring. Definitions come unstuck.

The *phrase* "sense of reality," in addition, is not as pointed as I would like. The man who fancies himself a realist swallows it with too little self-criticism. The word "myth," on the other hand, connotes "illusion" too powerfully. It is helpful to imagine that one's own sense of reality is, from someone else's standpoint or from a later standpoint of one's own, a myth. But one's own sense of reality is far from seeming to oneself like a form of illusion; quite to the contrary, it is as solid and certain a sense as one has—the very bastion of reality as against illusion. Still, we need a word that forces us to question even that sense; to question our fundamental criteria of relevance, evidence, perceptual arrangement, and decision; to question the framework, grid, *blik,* worldview by which we perceive, remember and project.

Sometimes the word "culture" seems more adequate, as when we speak of the peasant culture of Vietnam as opposed to the culture of American G.I.'s; the culture of blue collar workers as opposed to that of old Newport families; the neighbor culture of those whose signals for what is real and meaningful come from the folks around them as opposed to the book culture of those whose community of reality, meaning, and value is shared at longer range through the printed word. In the countryside of Vietnam, such is the power of the peasant culture, for example, that the orthodox Marxist story of the expropriation of the instruments of production by the proletariat made no sense until altered.[4] There is no proletariat in Vietnam, but there is in village culture an age-old struggle toward a community of achievement based on performance, a community spiritually attuned to "the Mandate of Heaven," a community which, even though modern, is close to the rhythms of the rice paddies, the mountains, and the sea.

Acts take place according to principles. Principles gain their concrete meaning from symbols. Symbols occur within stories. Stories have meaning within myths. The meaning of each lower level of discourse depends upon the meaning of each higher level. These dependencies may be illustrated.

The action, "The United States keeps its pledge to the

[4]John T. McAlister, Jr., and Paul Mus, *The Vietnamese and Their Revolution* (New York, 1970).

Government of South Vietnam and herewith dispatches 100,000 soldiers and supporting materiel," might exemplify several principles: (1) "keep pledges"; (2) "the interests of the United States require armed intervention"; (3) "communism—boo!" One action might exemplify several applicable principles at once, or one to the exclusion of others.

The principle, "keep pledges," might be observed under the symbolic background of the Boy Scout oath, the men of Thermopylae, bankers shaking hands, memories of Munich, the quiet feeling of a boy slipping a ring on his girl's finger, the imitation of the Dark Lady of Shalott, a Mississippi gambler, a traveling salesman in Nebraska, Machiavelli, Woodrow Wilson.

The symbol, "American flag," might be part of the story of the defense of the free world, or part of the story of a betrayal of American ideals. For many years Americans followed their flag in the defense of liberty; many now think that flag leads merely to the defense of world stability (a stability favorable to the U.S. standard of living).

The myth, "In some other world, we might do otherwise, but a harsh sense of reality compels us. . . ." provides a context within which a story has a determining meaning, a meaning which under another myth it might not have. Whose story about the outcome of the war in Vietnam seems realistic to President Nixon today? and how realistic does that story appear to the present successor of Ho Chi Minh? and which story will seem realistic to a majority of American commentators in the year 1990? which seemed realistic in 1960? The framework supplied by a sense of reality gives one story (or scenario) a cogency which another framework does not.

One can discover the contours of one's own sense of reality by noticing to which objects one applies words like "meaningful," "realistic," "reasonable," and "relevant." It is especially important to notice which human experiences one counts "real" enough to base one's actions on. For one's actions do not always have the same shape as one's rhetoric. Two senses of reality between which one oscillates may be in conflict.

In international politics, nations and even individual leaders often have quite different senses of reality. It follows under such conditions that all meanings lower on the scale are understood differently: what is "fact" to one is not to the other; "principles," even if similarly worded, may be differently understood; a conciliatory gesture may appear to another as a symbol of intransigence (Ho Chi Minh's letter to President Nixon, as revealed in Nixon's address of November 3, 1969?).

In domestic politics, the "radicalization" of white liberals is not merely the discovery of new facts or the acceptance of new principles, but a changed sense of reality, story, and symbols. The political conversion of Eldridge Cleaver, Malcolm X, and other blacks cannot adequately be stated in terms of principles and facts; hence their emphasis on non-pragmatic categories like "black consciousness," "soul," "revolutionary consciousness."

IV. TWO MODEST PROPOSALS

Foreign policy decisions, I now wish to argue, need to include concrete, critical attention both to the culture and to the story of the protagonists in the matters under decision. My proposals are twofold; but at present I can elaborate only the second.

The first proposal is as follows: *Do not assume that the American sense of reality is the same as that of the other nation or nations involved.* Put more strongly: *Do not assume that the American sense of reality is adequate to the dimensions of the problem.* The point of this proposal is, of course, to induce a natural sense of modesty. American officials often seemed confident that they understood what the issues were in Vietnam, what the aims and resolve and resources of the enemy were, and what the relevant course of action for America was. Americans tended to impose schemes and patterns upon the Vietnamese situation and to learn only slowly and at great cost (if at all) a flexibility of mind sufficient to come to grips with realities which proved much more refractory than anyone expected. The list of "mistakes" and "errors of judgment" is long. Much more important, a whole set of assumptions and criteria of evaluation has had to be challenged. Neither American officials nor commentators saw early the many ways in which American presuppositions and assumptions about Vietnam would lead the nation into a quagmire. Even David Halberstam's 1965 book[5] entitled with that metaphor, closed with an eloquent defense of the American involvement.

The American sense of reality, in its public presentation at least, tends to favor empiricism, facts, quantification, and as precisely a logical statement of goals and options and costs

[5] *The Making of a Quagmire* (Boston, 1965).

as possible. But this very sense of reality is, plainly, a bias.[6]

[6] The editors of *The Atlantic* have collected the studies on war in Vietnam which appeared in their pages in *Who We Are*, eds. Robert Manning and Michael Janeway (Boston, 1969). A paper included in that book first enjoyed underground circulation in Washington: "Minutes of a White House Meeting, Summer, 1967," by James C. Thompson, Jr. One refrain runs through those minutes—"Mr. Breslan . . . hoped that Mr. Ulan had taken a good hard look at the real numbers involved. He had always felt that numbers were important. Mr. Ulan said yes" (p. 43). "Mr. Breslan asked Mr. Gray to ride herd on this one. He hoped that they would take a good hard look at the real numbers involved" (p. 45 and *passim,* pp. 41-45).

In a more abstract way, General André Beaufre, former French commander in Indochina, gives a similar analysis of the American bias:

"The American Armed Forces are suffering from the same disease which struck the French Army after 1918: the disease of victory. Moreover, the consciousness of belonging to the mightiest and the richest nation in the world has aggravated the disease. Today the American Armed Forces believe that they know better than everybody else what is to be done, and that no lessons can be drawn from others' experience. They have no doubts about their doctrine and their own method of thought. (It seems to me that the Soviet Armed Forces suffer from the same disease, as far as I can judge from what I have seen of the Egyptian dispositions in the Sinai.)

"Now, the present dominant trend of American thinking puts the emphasis on material superiority, as did the French Army after 1918, forgetting that the measurable factors are only a part—and often a minimal part—of the overall problem. This leads to a strategy which tends to be more logistical than psychological or even operational, and which presupposes an overwhelming superiority. Moreover, this trend was reinforced by the development of nuclear strategy, where it seemed at first that material factors were absolutely dominant. But in the later stages, as the theory of deterrence evolved, psychological factors proved decisive. In fact, non-measurable factors constitute the essential part of strategy, whereas measurable factors are dominant only in tactics. Tactics must be the servants of strategy and not the reverse. And strategy must include *all* the factors, the military ones, of course, but also the political, psychological, economic, and diplomatic ones. It must be a 'total' strategy."

The bias leads us to give more weight to those things which can be counted, and to those things which can be reduced to logical schematizing, than to those factors which cannot be quantified or made verbally explicit. "Every quantitative measurement we have," Defense Secretary Robert McNamara used to like to say, "shows that we are winning the war." To designate such a bias as the exemplar of what constitutes "reasonable discourse" in politics is to choose too narrow a model. American business corporations tend to take too little notice of the impact of their way of thinking upon real, concrete human persons: upon themselves, their staff, their workers, their clients. They tend to deal abstractly—but effectively —with "economic considerations." "Hard-nosed" theory in academic life in the United States similarly favors a sense of reality that is highly selective. It has peculiar strengths and weaknesses.

An elaboration of this first proposal would take us into too long a discussion. Unquestionably, the sense of reality one adopts as one's own affects one's understanding of the stories one chooses to tell by one's life and by one's theories. (The role of the hard-nosed theoretician is not an easy one; long, rigorous practice is demanded.) Economy of discussion, however, may be best served by concentrating on the category "story" rather than on the category "culture," "sense of reality," or "myth."

My second proposal runs: *Before entering into a foreign policy commitment, American officials should answer three questions:* (1) *What is the story the United States wishes to tell in that part of the world?* (2) *What is the story the other nation in question wishes to tell?* (3) *What role can the United*

States best play in the story chosen by that other nation? (4) *What role can the other nation play in the United States story?* (5) *When conflicts in stories arise, how are they to be resolved?*

The point of this proposal is to bring to explicit attention the fact that the category "national interest" includes at least a twofold narrative form: a projection of past, present and future on the part of the United States, and a projection of past, present and future on the part of another nation. The phrase, "national interest," includes, therefore, a keen sensitivity to a possible, even highly probable, conflict of interpretive schemes. "National interest," sophisticated thinkers amply recognize, does not refer only to factors like economic resources, strategic defensive positions, and the like. It also refers to factors of the human spirit like credibility, prestige, loyalty, historical tradition, a set of national priorities. Among these latter factors, an awareness of possibly conflicting interpretations of history should also be included.

It is usual in American argument about Vietnam, among doves as among hawks, to leave the categories "sense of reality" and "story" out of account. David Little elaborates in his short monograph on the Vietnam debate an American scheme for understanding Vietnam. He structures his discussion around three points: (A) general American expectations for Vietnam fashioned from 1945-1953; (B) the general American perception of a threat to these expectations from about 1958 onward; (C) the realization of American expectations, and the need to establish standards of "how badly, or to what degree, we must lose."[7]

Specific debates "on the issues" tend to cluster around four

[7] *Op. cit.*, p. 75.

points: (1) whether North Vietnam committed "aggression" in South Vietnam; (2) whether the United States is acting within or outside international law in intervening in South Vietnam; (3) whether the North Vietnamese and the National Liberation Front represent the hope for a more liberal, or a less liberal, society in South Vietnam; and (4) whether the United States has any obligation, or any right, to intervene in the destiny of a nation like South Vietnam at all. Professor Little responds to the first two of these issues with special appendices, and to the last two by the accumulation of testimony throughout his argument.

These are taken to be the central, hard issues. The concrete conduct of the war is given a sub-heading. In a footnote, Professor Little remarks: "All of the observations [Robert MacAfee Brown, Mary McCarthy, Howard Zinn, and Neil Sheehan] make about the horrors of the war are terrifying. It is in cataloguing these things that the critics undoubtedly make their greatest impact upon sensitive people. Except for Sheehan, it is in discussing the other aspects of the Vietnam conflict that these authors are so much less persuasive or, let us say, are far more confident than they ought to be. They are, consequently, of little help to those who try to weigh and balance a number of conflicting considerations."[8]

Little next offers ten pages of reflection on the arguments concerning the strategic execution of the war. Most of his comments align him with "those generally sympathetic with the U.S. cause in Vietnam," among whom "there is fairly widespread rejection of the existing theory of victory held by the U.S. military—what [Herman] Kahn calls the 'attrition-

[8] *Ibid.*, p. 72, fn. 120.

pressure-ouch' theory."[9] Little concludes his discussion: "However one stands on these complicated strategic and tactical questions, it is clear that sorting out and reflecting on specific theories of victory (or theories of realistic expectation) is the level at which helpful discussion goes on."[10]

Little's discussion of the critics of the war is reasonably fair; and his defense of the U.S. position is reasonably typical. The structure he gives the entire discussion, I submit, exemplifies in sophisticated form the American manner of dealing with Vietnam. The heart of the matter comes first: Earlier policy, commitments and expectations; the threat of "aggression"; the legalities of intervention. In second place come instrumental matters: the actual strategy and tactics of the war. The argument is thus kept on the logical levels of principle and fact.[11] The problem of cross-cultural translation is by-

[9] *Ibid.*, p. 75.

[10] *Ibid.*, p. 83.

[11] Frances Fitzgerald's "The Struggle and the War: The Maze of Vietnamese Politics," *The Atlantic* (August, 1967), reprinted in *Who We Are,* op. cit., pp. 77-105, is the best achievement by an American of the jump from principle and fact to symbol, story, and myth. The following (pp. 78-79) suggests the gap:

"The United States is fighting a war in Vietnam on the basis of certain assumptions about the nature of Vietnam. That U.S. policy-makers have yearly had to revise their estimates about the course of the war and the need for American intervention raises the question of whether or not these assumptions conform to reality. Policy-makers assume, first, that the 17th parallel dividing North and South Vietnam corresponds to the frontier between East and West Germany in that it divides Vietnam into two parts, each of which has a separate identity. They assume that South Vietnam is a nation state, and that with a certain amount of assistance it can develop a non-Communist government which will satisfy the needs and aspirations of its population.

passed. Moreover, Little thinks in too flatly instrumentalist a way to notice the revelatory power of means: the choice of instruments gives the story away.

The *critics* of the war make the mistake of seeming to accept a logical structure like Little's. They attack the "myths" and "arrogance" which led to America's earlier policy commitments and expectations. They argue that "aggression" is not involved or, if involved, is no real threat to the United States; they decry the war as illegal. Since American public officials are generally believed trustworthy by the American people, the official position on these matters—which are not

In recent months President Johnson has offered to withdraw American troops from South Vietnam on the condition that North Vietnam withdraw its troops, presumably on the assumption that the South Vietnamese government could settle its own domestic problems were it not for Northern aggression. With these simple assertions the United States has drawn a design which does not correspond to the pattern of political forces in Vietnam. In 1962, Defense Secretary Robert McNamara said, 'Every quantitative measurement we have shows that we are winning the war.' His remark was a warning signal that the failure of prediction has not stemmed from mere over-optimism.

"To discuss solutions to Vietnamese problems it is first of all necessary to understand the problems as they occur to the Vietnamese. What is the relationship between man and society in Vietnam? What are the traditional modes of political expression, and how have they changed under the impact of the West? How do the Vietnamese view American policy and the American military presence?

"Culturally, as geographically, Vietnam is half a world away from the United States; an American travels to Vietnam only through a vast effort of translation." (Fitzgerald's note: "In attempting to give some notion of the categories of Vietnamese political thought, I am deeply indebted to Paul Mus, the French historain and anthropologist, born in Hanoi, who has done what I believe to be the only significant work on the subject. His *Sociologie d'une guerre* was published in 1952 during the Indochina War.")

black and white—carries virtually unimpeachable public weight. Hence the critics attack the daily strategy and tactics of the war; they hope thereby to reveal the unreality of the basic U.S. position. But, in fact, the revulsion of the critics against the war does not follow the logical structure outlined by Little. The critics, however, do not often recognize, still less define, the structure truly native to their argument. The category "story" illumines the area of disagreement, and the sources of revulsion.

Little reveals his own story when he writes: "To affirm the American moral creed is to adopt a point of view that makes it logically impossible to come to decisions exclusively on the basis of whether they contribute to the interests of the United States. The benefit of Americans is bound up with the benefit of 'all men.' "[12] He argues that both the Wilsonian tradition *and* the tradition of liberal disillusionment share that same creed. "The only serious difference arises over instrumental matters, over whether intervention or non-intervention is, as a rule, the most efficient means for attaining the shared end."[13]

Little elaborates: ". . . the fundamental 'moral qualities' of American life are not ethnic or nationalistic in character; the Declaration of Independence does not say 'all *American* men are created equal.' "[14] He quotes Robert Osgood approvingly: "If the . . . values which are the basis for America's social and political institutions *are valid at all, they are as*

[12] *Ibid.*, p. 89.

[13] *Ibid.*

[14] *Ibid.*, p. 86.

valid outside America's borders as within."[15] Little interprets Osgood's point as a logical point, "not simply Osgood's sentimental opinion." Thus America's concern for "an international environment compatible with its ideals and interests" is "a necessary extension of its peculiar national interest, namely, one that is defined in relation to a universalistic American creed."[16]

A man reveals the story he is living out both by his actions and by the metaphors he employs in his speech. To examine the logical category "story" in a man's writing is to look, first of all, at his key metaphors, either to those explicit metaphors which follow the words "like" and "as," or to those metaphors implicit in his words themselves (e.g., the way the word "implicit" has in it the metaphor "in-folded").

[15] *Ibid.*, p. 87, quoting Robert Osgood, *Ideals and Self-Interest in America's Foreign Policy* (Chicago, 1953), p. 125.

[16] *Ibid.*, p. 87. I don't think David Little recognizes how dangerous this story is. Compare the testimony of James C. Thomson, Jr., in "How Could Vietnam Happen?" in *Who We Are*, pp. 210-11:

"There is a final result of Vietnam policy I would cite that holds potential danger for the future of American foreign policy: *the rise of a new breed of American ideologues who see Vietnam as the ultimate test of their doctrine.* I have in mind those men in Washington who have given a new life to the missionary impulse in American foreign relations: who believe that this nation, in this era, has received a threefold endowment that can transform the world. As they see it, that endowment is composed of, first, our unsurpassed military might; second, our clear technological supremacy; and third, our allegedly invincible benevolence (our 'altruism,' our affluence, our lack of territorial aspirations). Together, it is argued, this threefold endowment provides us with the opportunity and the obligation to ease the nations of the earth toward modernization and stability: toward a full-fledged *Pax Americana Technocratica.*"

In Little's case, the governing metaphors are "creed" and "instrumental." America has a "peculiar national interest." Yes, peculiar, because it is a creed which apparently commits us to applying our own understanding of human life to the entire human universe: a national interest "that is defined in relation to a universalistic American creed." Professor Little *intends* by his discussion to prevent a merely cynical imposition of American values upon other people in the name of the mere national interest of the United States. So he defines the U.S. national interest in a universalistic way. But the logic of universals, and indeed of creeds, is not the logic of symbols, let alone the logic of stories or the logic of divergent senses of reality. To understand one's own national creed as universal, even when that national creed includes such universals as "freedom," "equality," "self-determination," and "justice," is far from modest. For universals gain their concrete meaning from symbols, stories, and myths. Apart from shared symbols, stories, and myths, such universals are certain to appear to others as foreign, strange, and even as manipulative.

Let me use one example from psychological warfare in Vietnam. While I was there,[17] an officer in operation WHAM ("Win the Hearts and Minds") described his program to me. Helicopters would descend without warning on a village that, in some cases, had never before seen Americans. A cordon would be drawn around the town. The men would be taken away for interrogation. The women and children would be gathered in the square to hear Navy musicians play rousing

[17] See also Orville Schell, "Cage for the Innocents," in *Who We Are*, pp. 130-46.

American band music. Frightened by strange music, surrounded by heavily armed and unusually large foreign-looking men, wondering what had become of their husbands and fathers, the women and children were smiled at and given objects they had never seen before. They were told to eat the strange-tasting objects, which they had no way of knowing were harmless U.S. gum and candy. A team of unarmed men then forced the children to line up, opened their mouths, prodded at their teeth with evil-looking instruments. Some youngsters they singled out; the men pulled out some teeth. A movie screen was set up. The people were exhorted by the strangers to be happy. They would not see any of the men of military age again. The Americans were tall, loud, and were conveyed in very noisy machines which blew great clouds of dust over everything inside the bamboo houses. They did not observe the quiet, subdued, elaborate manners of a Buddhist culture. They bribed the affections of children away from their parents, encouraged the children to be rowdy and outspoken.

The abstract principles, "better dental hygiene" and "friendly Americans" could scarcely be understood by Vietnamese peasants in the way Americans understood them. The Vietnamese had not seen the World War II pictures of American soldiers giving gum to children. They had seen Frenchmen, Japanese, and now Americans come through their village with military purpose. They worried whether they would be blamed by the Viet Cong company in the area—which had not been dislodged since the mid-1930's—for not resisting the surprise visit by the Americans. Artillery, bombs, and night attacks would be their lot until either the Americans or the Viet Cong went away.

But universals of far larger strategic importance than these are at stake in Vietnam. Is the American understanding of "equality" relevant to the actual, concrete conditions of life in the United States? What concrete meaning would "all men are created equal" have for Vietnamese ears? Do villagers in Vietnam wish to be considered equal to village chiefs, mandarin officials, Viet Cong officers, Buddhist monks? What do they imagine a noble life-story to be like? Do they imagine themselves to be members of a nation? (What is a nation? Why is the United States committed to "nation-building"—because no nation exists there?) What city would they answer is the capital of Vietnam? What emotional significance does the word "Hanoi" convey to them? What word do they use to describe the present conflict?

A strong case can be made that United States officials, academics and people know little or nothing about the people of Vietnam, about the symbols which move the Vietnamese to action, about the story the Vietnamese imagine themselves to be living out, about the sense of reality of Vietnamese officials, academics, and people. A strong case can be made that United States officials, academics and people *care* little about the symbols, stories or sense of reality of the Vietnamese. Less than ten thousand Americans in Vietnam speak Vietnamese, and most of those have a limited professional vocabulary and leave the country after one year. Very little visiting goes on between Americans and Vietnamese—for dinner, poetry, philosophy, long-range political-cultural interchange. The manners and customs of the Vietnamese are seldom even recognized, let alone respected. The Vietnamese person is thought of as underdeveloped, inferior, dumb, careless, untrustworthy, etc. It is difficult to think of a single Vietnamese philosopher, historian, poet, folk-singer, painter, social thinker, journalist, or cultural hero whose work is known, studied, and emulated in the United States. It is as if the symbols, stories, and sense of reality by which the Vietnamese understand their own dignity, value, and historical perspective simply do not exist for us—neither for our government officials, nor for our military men, nor for our academicians, nor for the American public generally.

Thus Americans are in the anomalous position of defending "equality," "freedom," "self-determination," and "justice" in a vacuum. They have almost no idea what symbols, stories, and sense of reality give such universals whatever concrete meaning they might have in Vietnamese life.

It is in this context that the use of enormous military fire power "to save American lives"—twice as much tonnage of explosives as was used in all of Europe and all of the Pacific Theatre in World War II—gets its profounder meaning. It is not just that as a "tactic" or "strategy" the use of heavy fire power is an incredibly stupid instrument in a guerrilla war. "It staggers belief," Sir Robert Thompson says of one small facet of the air war, the instructions given American helicopters to fire on any villages from which passing shots are fired on them.[18] It is also a strategy heedless of the realities of the Vietnamese flesh and spirit; there is a pattern of such heedlessness in the general American consciousness. It is a strategy of universals: making no allowance for symbolic values, the Vietnamese story in which it is being used, the general sense

[18] Quoted by Little, p. 77, from "Squaring the Error," *Foreign Affairs* (April, 1968), p. 453.

of reality (and proportion) of the Vietnamese people. As Sir Robert says: "This return fire reinforces every word the Viet Cong say, with the result that American intentions cease to be credible."[19]

Similarly, the strategy of General Westmoreland—"attrition-pressure-ouch"—was not widely objected to as a violation of the symbols, story, and sense of reality of the Vietnamese, both friendly and hostile. The history of Vietnam for at least the last hundred years is involved in the emotions behind the present war; the symbolic divisions in Vietnamese society are deep. Westmoreland's strategy was so gross and blundering as to be grotesque. The revulsion against war springs from the gap between the claim that the United States is in Vietnam to "defend the South Vietnamese" and to "build a nation" and a strategy of massive, indiscriminate, insensitive destruction. Westmoreland's story—"punish" the enemy until he says "uncle"—misses almost entirely the poignancy and complexity of what the Vietnamese refer to as "the struggle."

Both doves and hawks have shown appalling insensitivity to the way the Vietnamese view themselves and their history. Not comprehending the key Vietnamese stories, they are hardly prepared to define with sensitivity which role United States forces (motivated no doubt by a divergent, United States story) should adopt.

To avoid misunderstanding, my own opinions on Vietnam should no doubt be stated. I publicly supported the American military intervention in 1965, though with doubts about the conception of the war Americans might come to give rein to.[20]

19 *Ibid.*

20 My first articles appeared in *The National Catholic Reporter* during

U.S. intervention in 1965 could have played a role in Vietnamese history which Vietnamese themselves might have appreciated in their own terms. Further, I believe that the United States cannot morally withdraw from Vietnam without tending first to the military, political, economic, and cultural ill-effects a precipitate withdrawal might have. What went wrong in Vietnam was our massive disregard for the psychic tissue of Vietnamese culture: our insensitivity to Vietnamese conceptions of self-organization, group, family, religion, race, home, hearth, safety, justice, peace, equality, liberty. We were too certain of our own story: Defenders of the Free World, Punishers of Aggressors, Brandishers of Terrible Swift Swords. With the confidence of having universalist principles on our side, we ruthlessly disrupted homes, villages, and provinces in the name of our ideals, our conceptions, our methods.

In this respect, I do not find President Nixon's concept of "Vietnamization" comforting. George Orwell[21] taught us to

the summer of 1965. Later, in 1966, I wrote in the same place about my change of mind. A lengthier treatment of the change of mind appears in "Our Terrorism, Our Brutality," in *A Time to Build* (New York, 1968). A statement completed somewhat earlier appears as "Stumbling Into War and Stumbling Out," in *Vietnam: Crisis in Conscience* (New York, 1967). My reports from the field appeared during August and September, 1967, in *The National Catholic Reporter,* and further articles have appeared in *Commonweal.* Of possible special interest is my recommendation of a peace plan in *Commonweal* (October 10, 1969), pp. 45-47.

21 "In our time, political speech and writing are largely the defense of the indefensible. Things like the continuance of British rule in India, the Russian purges and deportations, the dropping of the atomic bombs on Japan, can indeed be defended, but only by arguments which are too brutal for most people to face, and which do not square with the professed aims of political parties. Thus political language has to con-

scrutinize carefully all political programs expressed in Latin words ending in "-ation": "pacification," "concentration camps," "liberation," etc. That Latin suffix is abstract and universalist; it covers everything. Heedless of concrete variety and individual flesh and blood, "Vietnamization" does not give "the struggle" of the Vietnamese people a concrete, Vietnamese meaning; it trains the army of General Thieu to prosecute American ideals by American methods with Vietnamese soldiers.

Americans are not sufficiently sensitive to what the Vietnamese find meaningful, relevant, reasonable, or real. They do not really have the hang of what makes the ordinary Vietnamese life—in Vietnamese terms—noble or ignoble, genuine or empty. And they do not know the subtleties and complexities of the Vietnamese national stories; how the Vietnamese interpret their own past and their own present, and how they project (and how they probably cannot; from sensitive Vietnamese I hear only cries of despair) their own future. In such almost total human ignorance, how can Americans be so presumptuous as to carry out the physical and cultural destruction they have wreaked? It is the wedding of ignorance and a massively destructive strategy that I find (on traditional "just war" grounds) immoral. Our end is unclear (to protect

sist largely of euphemism, question-begging, and sheer cloudy vagueness. Defenseless villages are bombarded from the air, inhabitants driven out into the countryside, the cattle machine-gunned, the huts set on fire with incendiary bullets; this is called *pacification*. Millions of peasants are robbed of their farms and sent trudging along the roads with no more than they can carry; this is called *transfer of population* or *rectification of frontiers*. A mass of Latin words falls upon the facts like snow, blurring the outlines and covering up all the details."

the Vietnamese, yes, but who they are and what their reality is we do not know). Our means are grossly destructive and irreversible—you cannot later bring the dead back to life and apologize to them for errors involved in the original lack of discrimination.

The revulsion against the war in Vietnam stems from the gross insensitivity of our intervention, not an insensitivity of the feelings but of our intelligence and our methods of understanding people and politics. Many of those who oppose the war are not pacifist. They support wars and revolutions for the cause of freedom, justice, equality. There is sufficient reason to believe they would willingly suffer physical pain, oppression or death in such causes. They do not lack for zeal, ardor, or ideological singlemindedness. But the symbol of the American soldier in Vietnam, and the story told by the American army in Vietnam, suddenly crossed over and merged for many into the war-comics symbol of the well-armed Nazi following orders, and the story of indiscriminate, large-scale ruthlessness in the name of empire.

No one knows the names of the Vietnamese, or the faces—certainly not their symbols and stories. Hence, many intuitively know, we cannot be in Vietnam for the sake of the Vietnamese, but for our own version of righteousness: as it happens this time, a realist's righteousness.

V. TRUE STORIES, FALSE STORIES

The American bias suggests that modern nations have moved from a worldview composed of myth, story and symbol to a worldview of empirical reason, fact, and verification—from myth to reality. So deep is the bias of demythologizing that Americans fail to notice how problematic is their own relationship to nature, to one another, to other peoples, to their own bodies and emotions. The acceptance of a worldview composed of a sort of social darwinism and scientific consciousness does strange things to the way people walk, talk, think of themselves, act in the human community. It is not self-evident that the American character, statistically or in significant individuals, represents a higher type of human being than the world has seen before. It is not self-evident that American intelligence, whether in the academic, political or business community, presents a more humane, moral and progressive face to the world than that of other cultures in the past.

Still, the category "story" is in itself neutral. The words "account," "narrative," "historical record" could perhaps do as well. The point of the category as applied to politics is the power of narratives to engender sequences of actions by linking them in meaningful sequences—not only conceptually meaningful, but also psychically meaningful. A story is the logical category by which a person achieves a sense of "belonging" to a group or "being faithful" to himself. It is distinguishable from a principle, strategy, or policy because those are conceptual tools, abstract, capable of supporting many variant styles of action. A story is a linking of concrete imaginative symbols. It may, to be sure, be summarized in an abstract plot-line: "The Marxist story is the expropriation of the instruments of production by the proletariat." But the actual story is the concrete account of 1917—either as sheer, factual history in all its detail or, more often, in the shortened but heightened form that memory gives complexity.

A story may link events which have not yet occurred with those which have, e.g., a future condition of blessedness with present deeds in the midst of struggle. What is essential to story is its capacity to interpret and to link otherwise variant experiences and actions, to focus action and often to inspire it. George Wallace and Robert F. Kennedy often appealed to the same lower middle-class white voters in 1968, interpreting and shaping the alienation they found there along quite different lines. Ho Chi Minh meditated long on the life of the Vietnamese peasant before he felt certain how to link their experiences with Marxist themes.

The critical question must also be faced. How do I go about telling a true story from a false one? How are stories linked to facts, principles, and other logical categories? In Vietnam, according to McAlister and Mus,[22] the peasant waits for a sign of heaven's favor before he accepts a political story as true. If social institutions are out of harmony with natural rhythms, and if men are restless and disordered, the Vietnamese wait for a new regime to link the social order once again with the natural order. The new regime must promise spiritual reconciliation of the social with the natural, and also show by its practical success that heaven blesses it. The criteria are both spiritual and pragmatic.

How do people in the United States tell a true story from a false one? How did they come to accept the restructuring of American symbols, groups, and sequences of action adroitly achieved by Richard Nixon in his campaign in 1968 and in

[22] "The Mandate of Heaven: Politics as Seen From the Vietnamese Village," in *The Vietnamese and Their Revolution,* chapter 3. See also "The Peasant Politics of Wait-and-See," pp. 122-27, and p. 150.

his first year of office? (Think how easily he threw the triumphant peace movement of October 15, 1969, into disarray by November 15.) How did Americans come to accept the costs of the unpopular Vietnam war as a part of the American story, credible and supportable? Those who are in touch with the many stories of America which are still capable of focusing and inspiring action have in their hands one of the main criteria by which, in fact, stories are judged for their truth: consonance with stories held in the past. It is seldom enough that an individual is so totally converted that he loses all vestiges of his former life story, and lives according to a totally new one. It is almost impossible for whole groups to undergo such transformation; even to do so within the span of two or three generations requires enormous social dislocations. The story of modernization—of urbanization, rationalization, bureaucratization, industrialization—runs head-on into the peasant society's story of past, present, and future, jars its sense of time, purpose, organization, uproots the individual from an age-old story.

Stories are judged by consonance with past stories, by their ability to account for facts and experiences, by their power to inspire actions, by their effectiveness in producing benefits for a society or a person, by the feeling of reconciliation they bring, by the plausibility and attractiveness of the future they portend, sometimes by their complexity and flexibility. What, for example, makes the Christian story credible or incredible? Or the story of science, enlightenment, and progress? And what brings about a "failure of nerve"?

Among recent political writings, John McAlister's already cited *The Vietnamese and Their Revolution,* derived from

Paul Mus' *Sociologie d'une guerre,* is an almost flawless example of attention to the categories of culture, story, and symbol. In the "cultural shock" of the Vietnamese war, Americans have an unparalleled opportunity to discover the limits of their own culture, story, and symbols. To read McAlister and Mus is to be able, again and again, to notice, to interpret, or to reconcile countless vagrant experiences and baffling occurrences of the last ten years of the war. So many matters suddenly *make sense.* Whereas so long as we talk merely about principles and facts the American effort *should* make sense, but doesn't.

Why is it that large numbers of Vietnamese have not gone over to the Viet Cong? Why is it that many Vietnamese looked, hopefully at first, to the French and later to the Americans as agents of heaven who might restore a lost cosmic order? Why is it that the Vietnamese are rapidly disillusioned by contact with Americans—why American ideals and character traits do not win esteem? Why is it that "their" Vietnamese, as one U.S. colonel put it, fight so much better than "our" Vietnamese? Why is it that young Vietnamese officers rapidly learn contempt for American perception, sensibility, and understanding? Why is it that the Saigon regime has strength in cities, and generates new cities and slums all over the land, while unable to generate initiative and loyalty in the countryside? Why is it that the economy of Vietnam grinds so unevenly—even independently of the war—on countryside and on city? In what ways did the Marxist sense of reality, story, and symbols have to be radically changed by Ho Chi Minh in order to enter into the Vietnamese sense of reality, story, symbols? What in the American sense of reality renders Americans imperceptive to the exigencies of "political warfare"?

McAlister and Mus establish the Vietnamese sense of reality.[23] What is real is connected to the stars and the entire cosmos; what is real brings order, strength, reconciliation, and ends disorder and inner restlessness; what is real is communal, and ties not only individuals but also villages and whole nations together into a virtually cosmic community; what is real allows each person to participate and to exercise his own skills in building up the communal project; what is real has the quiet power and inner peace of ordered rice paddies, seasons, laws of growth. Technical, external, disruptive, confused, non-communitarian efforts are unreal, destructive, unworthy of support, out of contact with the heavens and the earth. The village and its values are the chief criteria of the real, the reasonable, the meaningful, and the relevant.

The Vietnamese story[24] is the story of a "struggle" (com-

[23] *Ibid.,* "Prologue" and "The Political Consequences of Vietnamese Concepts of Society," chapter 5, pp. 78-92.

[24] "The explanation . . . of why a peasant people with a deep sense of spirituality would become committed to mass participation in a national movement that was more overtly political than any in their previous history is the story of revolution in Vietnam. It is also the reason for this book" (p. 4). In his "Epilogue: The Meaning of the Revolution in Viet Nam" (pp. 155-66), McAlister uses the word "values" and "cultural differences" where I would want to distinguish sense of reality, story, symbol. (My reason is that many American academics think of values as principles chosen according to different priorities; but McAlister means something more concrete and dense than that, involving concrete experience and imagination and inclination.) McAlister writes: "But values are more than principles for personal conduct; they are also sources of social cohesion and guides for social action. Without common values men find it difficult to work together toward common goals. They either don't trust each other or

plicated, laden Vietnamese word) to bring about a new cosmic order, according to which the society of the village can enter a new chapter of its life, brought into the modern world order but without being destroyed thereby. A modern economy of highways, railroads, and airports cannot be sustained by a decentralized village economy; the taxation required is unfair unless villagers have access, not only to a barter economy, but also to modern currency. And the villagers need some way to participate, with full talent, energy, and advancement, in the revolution that would tie their villages into the modern cosmic whole. The Viet Cong measure a villager's skill by his knowledge and his practice of the revolutionary struggle, and promote him accordingly; the Saigon government has more trouble entrusting the villagers with weapons, or counting on them for leadership. For the Saigon regime is urban, modern, Western, and out of touch with the villagers' sense of reality. As Vietnamese, it holds the Viet Cong at bay; as Western and urban, it lacks spirituality as much as the Viet Cong.

The symbols[25] which catalyze action for the Vietnamese are those of the village; of the nation Vietnam and its century-

they don't understand each other. Words don't have the same meaning to people who have different values" (p. 156). I would substitute the more concrete notion of "story" and "sense of reality" for the word "values" in these sentences—"story" for the first occurrence, and "sense of reality" for the next two. It would be better, of course, to expand the sentences briefly to speak precisely of symbol, story, sense of reality —and, in place of "words," "words describing principles, words describing facts."

25 "The Traditional Symbols of Vietnamese Politics," in *ibid.*, pp. 62-65 and *passim*.

old "struggle" for cultural autonomy; of world order; of harmony with oxen, rice paddies, mountains, the dove—the quiet village dove of natural grace, natural order, times of community. Marxist symbols clash with Vietnamese symbols by their lack of spirituality, their economic reductionism. American symbols clash with Vietnamese symbols by their urban sense of reality, massive, technical, bureaucratic, external, impersonal.

The way even the best-intentioned Americans think, feel, and perceive is characteristically at odds with Vietnamese thinking, feeling, perceiving. The dissonance occurs not so much at the level of fact or policy as at the prior levels of sense of reality, story, and symbols, which are the context and base for fact and policy. The American sense of fact, and American principles, policies, and strategies, float in the air without touching ground in Vietnam, out of touch with the social web, the cultural matrix, the psychical tissue of Vietnamese life. That is what makes the war so surreal, so nightmarish, so brutal, and finally so inhumane. Men are not dealing with real men, but with abstract and elusive shadows of one another.

VI. A PLANETARY POWER

For better or worse, the American nation is the wealthiest (both in goods and in technology) and most powerful on this planet. In a technological era, there is no neutral political spot. Non-intervention is now as influential on world affairs as intervention. Everything the United States does, and does not do, affects the health, well-being and survival of real people elsewhere on the globe. For conditions of security, poverty, famine and disease still afflict a majority of human beings. It is idle, then, to argue for or against a non-interventionist foreign policy.

The overriding question is how persons from one national culture can come to understand people in other national cultures, in order to know what role to play in their history. All national stories are slowly becoming inextricable subplots in one planetary story.

To meet this problem merely on the logical level of principles, policy, strategy—of universals—is to court disaster. The way of abstractions, as Sartre and Camus learned from the experience of their generation, is the way of destruction. American liberalism (like the Enlightenment) has been "progressive" precisely by its willingness to weigh universal principles more heavily than concrete local "prejudices" or "myths"; it has found science a useful political ally in this demythologization of local powers. Thus the lesson of renewed respect for concrete differences will be a hard one to learn. Still, it is well known that the French *liberté* does not have the same meaning as the American *freedom;* nor, in English, does *liberty* (as in "Civil Liberties Union") have the same meaning as freedom (as in Young Americans for Freedom"). "Equality" does not have the same significance for blacks in the United States as for whites; for blue-collar workers as for publishers and editors. "Justice" does not carry with it the same historical expectations in a Vietnamese village as in, say, Dallas or even Junction City. Foreign policy goals stated as principles ("self-determination," "freedom," "peace with honor") are forms of semantic imperialism. Political theory, therefore, needs to give systematic attention to categories of inquiry which unmask the abstractness of pragmatism and realism; but without necessarily giving comfort to the local status quo.

The cure for a parochialism disguised by the pretension of universality is an explicit, critical awareness of the concrete contours of one's own experience. For that experience has been shaped by particular, concrete symbols and stories, and by a concrete sense of reality. Also required is a critical map of the concrete contours of the experience of men in other nations, shaped by different symbols and stories and by a different sense of reality. Finally, we need methods for leading other persons into our own sense of reality, to see our story from our viewpoint; and methods whereby we may be similarly led into theirs.

Conflicts between senses of reality, and conflicts between stories, are not as easy to resolve as conflicts over principles or facts. For the former supply the criteria in whose light the latter are arrived at. Arguments concerning criteria of evidence, relevance, and meaningfulness are dialectical, indirect, subtle. Rather than at logical rigor or analytic precision, they aim at generating a conversion, a fresh standpoint, a new sympathy "from within." It is a great strength of Western culture to try to bring as many matters into the clear light of principles and facts as possible. It was an ancient part of the same Western wisdom to invent ways of pushing one's inquiries also into those more obscure areas which the clear light of direct analysis cannot be made to penetrate. American realism has tended to prefer the narrow circle of light.

There is no one single form of human reason, because

there is no one single language, no one set of images, no one same realm of historical experience. To deal with the diversity of the human race, the concrete logic of imagination and sensitivity[26] is a more reliable guide for intelligence than the abstract logic of principles, means and ends. The latter tends inherently to superimpose one same way of viewing the world on everything. The former tends inherently to promote a different response to each culture, each nation and each person.

To think of asking, "What is the story which nation X thinks it is living out?" is a good device for deciding which role to play in a foreign policy decision involving nation X. To develop an accurate phenomenology of stories operative in international politics today would be a great service to political intelligence. It would, for one thing, decisively complicate the two-story view of the universe which inspires the cold war. It would promote respect for ethnic and other minority values. And it would open new possibilities to the realism which in America is now in disarray.

[26] Four authors are of special use in beginning to work out a theory of symbol, story and myth for political contexts: Murray Edelman, *The Symbolic Uses of Politics* (Urbana, Ill., 1967); Hugh Dalziel Duncan, *Symbols in Society* (New York, 1968); and Kenneth Burke and Harold Lasswell in their several works.

THE FOUNDATION OF MAN

Tran Van Dinh

Long before the Christian era, the Confucians in China and in Vietnam proclaimed their faith in the goodness of man, and believed that "all men in the four seas are brothers." Assuming now, twenty-five centuries later, that in "a technological era there is no neutral political spot" and that "non-intervention is now as influential on world affairs as intervention" (Novak), then the history of U.S. commitment-intervention in Vietnam (1950-54, on the side of the colonial French; 1954-present time, on the side of the anti-Communist Vietnamese) has indeed been clearly characterized by innocent ignorance and/or tragic misunderstanding and/or arrogant disregard of Vietnamese "stories." From 1945 until 1954, the Vietnamese "story" was that of anti-colonialism, national independence. From 1954 until the present, the story has been enlarged to include, besides nationalism, territorial unity (reunification) and social revolution, which can be catalogued as "story projection of the future" (Novak). National independence and territorial unity are "records of the past" (Novak again). The U.S. policy-makers of the cold war took a story projection of the future—in this case the application of Marxism-Leninism in the development of the Vietnamese society, the use of Marxist dialectics in the re-interpretation of Buddhism, Confucianism, Taoism in the context of twentieth-century Vietnam—as an actual, fundamentally dangerous and threatening story and reacted accordingly (see my article, "The Other Side of the Table," in the *Washington Monthly* of January, 1970).

Besides stories there are sub-stories or historical events re-erupting and developing from general stories. Sub-stories often change the whole spectrum of political life for a period of time, because their emergence helps relate the masses to a "story-record of the past" and thus create unity of action. One of the best sub-stories one can use for illustration is the Buddhist Crisis in South Vietnam in the summer of 1963, which dramatically changed the whole political-psychological-military complex of South Vietnam and altered profoundly the course of U.S. policy and its military strategy in the whole of Vietnam. On Monday, June 11, 1963, at the intersection of Phan Dinh Phung and Le Van Duyet,[1] two busy streets in Saigon, a 72-year-old Buddhist monk named Thich Quang Duc burned himself "to call the attention of the world public to the sufferings of the Vietnamese people under Ngo Dinh Diem's oppressive regime." As Thich Nhat Hanh, a Buddhist monk who has lectured extensively in this country and now lives in Paris, wrote about the event:

> The Venerable Thich Quang Duc's self-immolation had a far greater emotional impact on the West then on the East

[1] Phan Dinh Phung (1847-1895) is a hero of the early Vietnamese resistance against the French colonization. Le Van Duyet (1763-1832) was a Vietnamese Field Marshal whose temple, "Lang Ong," is on the outskirts of Saigon. He once engineered the installation of a Cambodian Quisling—Nac Ong Chan—on the throne of Cambodia.

because of the great difference in religious and cultural backgrounds.[2]

Despite its great emotional impact, mainly conveyed through the mass media, the sub-story was not properly understood in the United States—understood, that is, against the Vietnamese Buddhist background. Government officials were scurrying to libraries to find books on Vietnamese Buddhism written in English, and none existed. Newspapers used the word "suicide" to describe the monk's self-immolation, giving it a totally different meaning in a Christian country which saw self-burning as "an act of savagery, violence and fanaticism, requiring a condition of mental imbalance." In a letter to Martin Luther King, Thich Nhat Hanh explained:

> The self-burning of Vietnamese Buddhist monks in 1963 is somehow difficult for the Western Christian conscience to understand. The press spoke then of suicide, but in essence it is not. It is not even protest. What the monks said in the letters they left before burning themselves aimed only at alarming, at moving the hearts of the oppressors, and at calling the attention of the world to the suffering endured then by the Vietnamese. To burn oneself by fire is to prove that what one is saying is of the utmost importance. There is nothing more painful than burning onself. To say something while experiencing this kind of pain is to say it with utmost courage, frankness, determination and sincerity. During the ceremony of ordination, as practiced

[2] *Viet Nam: Lotus in a Sea of Fire* (New York, 1967), p. 1. In *Foreign Affairs* (January, 1970), Henry A. Kissinger, assistant to President Nixon on national security affairs, wrote: "It would be difficult to imagine two societies less meant to understand each other than the Vietnamese and the American."

in the Mahayana tradition, the monk-candidate is required to burn one or more small spots on his body in taking the vow to observe the 250 rules of a bhikshu, to live the life of a monk, to attain enlightenment, and to devote his life to the salvation of all beings. . . . The Vietnamese monk, by burning himself, says with all his strength and determination that he can endure the greatest of sufferings to protect his people. But why does he have to burn himself to death? The difference between burning oneself and burning oneself to death is only a difference in degree, not in nature. A man who burns himself too much must die The importance is not to take one's life, but to burn. What he really aims at is the expression of his will and determination, not death. In the Buddhist belief, life is not confined to a period of 60 or 80 or 100 years: life is eternal. Life is not confined to this body: life is universal. To express will by burning oneself, therefore, is not to commit an act of destruction but to perform an act of construction, that is, to suffer and to die for the sake of one's people. This is not suicide. Suicide is an act of self-destruction, having as causes the following: (1) lack of courage to live and to cope with difficulties; (2) defeat by life and loss of all hope; (3) desire for nonexistence (abhaya). This self-destruction is considered by Buddhism as one of the most serious crimes. The monk who burns himself has lost neither courage nor hope; nor does he desire nonexistence. . . .

The sub-story of the Buddhist crisis is related in the minds and hearts of Vietnamese to the story of the close relationship between *Dao Phap* (religion) and *Dan Toc* (nation), of the historical contribution of Buddhism in the building of Vietnamese culture—especially during the golden age of Buddhism from the eleventh to fifteenth centuries, when Vietnam prospered—and to a larger story of the East that "philosophy was not distinctly separated from religion: they were both intimately related to one's social life."[3]

The larger story of Vietnam is that of the country's 4,000-year-long history itself, a history which was both a continuity and a series of revolutions, a history determined by the myth of the birth of the Vietnamese race, molded and nurtured by three currents of religions and/or philosophies—Buddhism, Confucianism, Taoism[4]—conditioned by the 800-year-long *Nam Tien* (March to the South), structured by the Vietnamese concepts of the Mandate of Heaven, of *Cach Menh* (revolution), of the creation of new communities and villages (*Xa*)—the latter "not as political acts but as spiritual ones"[5]—and, finally, a history sustained by the truly socialist nature of the Vietnamese society itself (socialism in Vietnamese is *Chu Nghia Xa Noi,* or the Doctrine of the Association of Villages).

The myth of the birth of the Vietnamese race goes back to the misty Bronze Age during which De Minh (a great grandson of Than Nong, the God of Agriculture) met, in the course of one of his inspection tours in the southern part of China, a *Tien* (fairy), and married her. From this union a

3 Dr. D. T. Suzuki, in *The Status of the Individual in East and West,* ed. Charles A. Moore (Honolulu, Hawaii, 1964), p. 519.

4 In the words of Dr. Thomas F. Fang: "To the Confucians, the individual should be ceaselessly edified; to the Taoists, he should be constantly liberated; and to the Buddhists he should be perpetually purified. . . ." *Ibid.,* p. 24.

5 Paul Mus and John T. McAlister, *The Vietnamese and Their Revolution* (New York, 1970), p. 4.

son, Loc Tuc, was born. And when De Minh was too old to rule his vast empire, he divided it into two territories: the North, which he gave to his eldest son, De Nghi, child of his first marriage, and the South (Vietnam), which he gave to Loc Tuc. Loc Tuc became Emperor Kinh Duong Vuong and married the daughter of Than Long (the Dragon God). From this marriage between the descendant of a fairy and a dragon there came a son who would be Emperor Lac Long Quan. Indeed, the Vietnamese often call themselves "the children and grandchildren of a dragon and a fairy." Lac Long Quan's marriage to Au Co, another fairy, resulted in the birth of one hundred male children. He told his wife one day: "I came from the race of Rong (Dragon), you came from the race of Tien. We are as different as water is to fire, and it would be unwise for us to continue to live together. We have to part." Fifty children then followed their mother to the mountains and fifty marched with their father to the south seas (a literal translation of fatherland in Vietnamese is *Giang Son,* or rivers and mountains). Lac Long Quan then handed over his throne to his son, Rung Vuong, who founded the Rong Bang Dynasty and named his kingdom Van Lang.,

The last Rong Bang Emperor (all are still remembered and celebrated as founding fathers in both North and South Vietnam on the tenth day of the third month of the lunar calendar) had a daughter of rare beauty. He had refused to give her hand in marriage to the neighboring King of Thuc for fear of the latter's territorial ambitions, but then two powerful Gods—Son Tinh (God of the Mountains) and Thuy Tinh (God of the Water) appeared simultaneously and asked to marry the Emperor's daughter. Faced with a very difficult choice, for both were equally strong and handsome, the Emperor decided that the God who would bring first the traditional wedding presents would have his daughter. Son Tinh returned at dawn the next day and took his bride away to the mountains. The angry loser, Thuy Tinh, resorted to his weapons, wind and water, to destroy his rival. But Son Tinh fought back fiercely with deadly thunder strikes. Defeated, Thuy Tinh retreated temporarily to the high seas. (But every year since then, between the sixth and seventh months, the duel has been renewed and Vietnam becomes the battleground of the two giants.) The King of Thuc, who had earlier been denied the hand of the beautiful princess of Van Lang, attacked the kingdom. Unprepared, the last Emperor of Rong Bang Dynasty (which had ruled for more than 2,600 years, from 2879 to 258 B.C.) was beaten and commited suicide.

Thuc Phan, the victorious Thuc king, merged his own kingdom with the conquered Van Lang, created a new country named Au Lac, and became Emperor An Duong Vuong. An Duong Vuong built his capital, Loa Thanh, in the form of a shell, with the help of God Kim Guy (Golden Tortoise), who gave him a miraculous claw. Mounted on a crossbow, the claw became a magic weapon which repulsed all foreign armies—in particular, that of the Chinese, headed by Trieu Da. The Chinese warlord offered to make peace with An Duong Vuong, but was in reality looking for revenge. Simulating a gesture of friendship, Trieu Da demanded and received the hand of An Duong Vuong's daughter, Princess My Chau, for his son, Trong Thuy. But when Trong Thuy had become a trusted member of the An Duong family, at the suggestion of his father he made plans to steal the miraculous claw.

This accomplished, Au Lac was attacked by the Chinese and An Duong Vuong, deprived of his magic weapon, was defeated. He fled to the seas on horseback with his daughter My Chau to implore the assistance of the Golden Tortoise. The God appeared and told him: "Your enemy is on your back." Realizing his family had betrayed him, and in a moment of desperate rage, An Duong Vuong killed My Chau. With a rhinoceros horn in his hands, An Duong Vuong then vanished with Golden Tortoise in the deep blue sea. Trong Thuy brought his wife's body back to the capital for burial, but, chagrined and consumed by guilt, he threw himself into a well where My Chau had often come to sit and listen to bird songs. The blood spilled from My Chau's body when she was beheaded by her father at the seaside was absorbed by oysters and transformed into pearls. When washed and cleansed with the water of the well where Trong Thuy died, the pearls acquired a remarkable brilliance. The two were thus finally reconciled in death.

From this recital of legendary origins, one can see that Vietnam considers its fate determined by:

1. A contradiction—the marriage between the descendant of a fairy (sweet, gracious, beautiful) and a dragon (powerful, aggressive, and hard-featured). These two contradictory aspects still prevail both physically and mentally in the Vietnamese people, and especially among the women who are slender but tough, durable and aggressive but romantic and gracious. The fairy virtues seem to be most apparent and persistent, however. (It might be noted here that in 1967 the North Vietnamese armies chose to fight the U.S. Marines in conventional battles at Con Tien [Hill of the Fairy—and *not*

Con Thien, as was mentioned in the American press] at the 17th Parallel. Perhaps the North Vietnamese wanted to show that they are worthy of their Mother Fairy.)

2. An internal division—the first Vietnamese family was a divided one (fifty children went with their mother to the mountains and fifty accompanied their father to the seas). Division and disunity became Vietnamese national problems in the past as well as at the present time. And the division is not only between North and South but also between the minorities which live in the mountains (Montagnards) and the majority dwelling in the *pallins* of the sea coasts. In North Vietnam, the minorities problem was practically solved by the creation of "autonomous areas" and by a sincere effort to respect the minorities' cultures. In South Vietnam, the problem remains unsolved and the Montagnards, still referred to as *Moi* (savages), are looked down upon and denied a meaningful participation in national affairs—except in areas controlled by the Provisional Revolutionary Government of South Vietnam and the National Liberation Front (N.L.F.). As for the territorial reunification of the two Vietnams, it is still the deepest aspiration of all Vietnamese.

3. A constant awareness and vigilance against possible invasions by foreign countries which attempt to foment internal divisions and use Vietnamese traitors for their territorial ambitions—and from this a fierce determination to defend the fatherland, a cause hard fought since earliest times. The Vietnamese have also learned that an enemy of Vietnamese national independence is also a promoter of territorial division.

4. An existence marred by social injustices and misfortunes imposed by superior and often outside forces. To survive, the

Vietnamese had to hide their true identity, to be both like and different from the enemy. Fishermen at first, the Vietnamese tattooed their bodies to frighten the sea devils and also to look like crocodiles (and this custom persisted until the reign of Emperor Tran Anh Tong (1293-1314). The N.L.F. soldiers today and the Vietminh soldiers of the 1950's are known for their expertise in camouflage. And the Vietnamese people are eager to learn foreign languages and to penetrate the foreign cultures which attempt to dominate them in order to know the foreigners better, the better to combat them. They are not xenophobic, but they cannot afford to completely trust the foreigners. They know that they have been victims of conflicts which often are irrelevant to the national interests. Once a battleground for the God of Mountains and the God of Water, today the cold war between the Communists and the "Free World" is being fought on their soil. Vietnamese are secure only behind the bamboo screens of their villages.

In this sanctuary, which they have slowly built with their hands, their sweat, their blood and their tears, surrounded by their elders and selected leaders, their *Dinh* (community center) and their *Chua* (Buddhist temple), the Vietnamese organize their life, edify their civilization, sharpen their culture, develop their humor, compose their *Ca Dao* (folk song or free song). Village life is not easy of course. It is a constant battle, but the battle is accepted and is fought with a Confucianist methodology, a Buddhist perspective, and a Taoist liberating spirit—in short, with optimism and patience. From the green ricefields sandwiched between majestic mountains and generous oceans grew a deep sense of romanticism; from the common sufferings and the common joy emerged an incurable optimism which brought in laughter and confidence. And why not? Even if men cannot be trusted, there is still the kind and hard-working water buffalo, the most faithful companion of the peasants. Premier Pham Van Dong of North Vietnam used to tell foreign journalists that "we Vietnamese revolutionaries are romantic and optimistic." He meant to say that Vietnamese revolutionaries are the true sons and daughters of the Vietnamese land.

Prisoners of a fate conditioned by internal divisions, by fear of foreign domination, by a deep consciousness of social injustices, the Vietnamese—confident and optimistic, persistent and romantic—patiently struggle to change their implacable destiny, and thus engage in revolutions. Revolution in Vietnamese is *Cach Menh,* or the change of human condition (or fate)—or, in more precise language, the change of the Mandate of Heaven from which political authority is established and entrusted in the hands of the people with a just cause and as a reward for their struggle.

View American actions in Vietnam against this story, with all its meanings and messages. One can see that the root of the failure of U.S. policy in Vietnam was the attempt, with massive amounts of money and guns, to create out of a Vietnamese revolution—albeit Communist in inspiration and leadership—an anti-Communist crusade which led Washington to support a "clique" of Vietnamese who are, by past political deeds, education and training, the least Vietnamese of all. They are the soldiers (and soldiers are ranked last in the Vietnamese hierarchy of values, which ranges as follows: *Si* [scholars, intellectuals], *Nong* [peasants], *Cong* [workers], *Thuong* [merchants], *Binh* [soldiers]), paid in the past by the French and now by the Americans to fight for an essentially anti-national cause.

Certainly in invading Cambodia with U.S. and South Vietnamese troops, the United States stepped into another unknown story, into a civilization very different even from that of the Vietnamese, one more Hinduized than Sinocized, a civilization best represented by the wonders that are the Angkor temples.

> The difference between the principles of Khmer aesthetics and ours is obvious. Our own buildings are reared in affirmation of the ascendancy of man. They compel the landscape to obey their own law, using natural features the better to exhalt themselves. They are designed in defiance of all restraint, bestriding or eviscerating or imprisoning nature in formal gardens filled with hardy plants and gushing fountains. Whence it comes that from the marching Greek columns to the flights of Gothic architecture, it is the vertical that predominates. But in Cambodia, everything is different. It is not that mankind has sunk to lower level: it has learnt humility. Like the embankment of the rice fields fitting closely to the contours of the land or the villages strung along the river bank, the temple outlining the horizon crouches on the soil from which it derives its magic power. When, as sometimes happens, it stands erect, it is noticeable how it rises by successive tiers with terrace piled on terrace, knowing nothing of the springing arch or vault. Furthermore, its sole raison d'etre is to reproduce the sacred mountain, handiwork of the Gods themselves. It is a magic diagram traced on the parchment of the plain, visible only from

above, decipherable in fact only by the immemorial Gods for whom it was built.[6]

The mythical message of the Vietnamese story was carried to its people by the Dragon and the Fairy. In Cambodia, it is the Garuda (a bird) and the Naga (a serpent). Thus the Indochina war becomes the story of a duel between the American Eagle on the one side, and on the other side, the Dragon and the Fairy, the Bird and the Serpent.

To choose Vietnam and Cambodia as examples is to demonstrate American ignorance of the stories of these two countries, an ignorance which is leading America to a course of action which will prove to be disastrous even if temporary military achievements can be obtained. But in the U.S. itself, what stories led to the adoption of this course of action? (The *implementation* of policy is related to other nations' stories, but, in seeking reasons for *adoption* of a policy, the initiating country's own stories are the principal issue.) It can be said that the decision to intervene in Vietnam in the 1950's was made because of four central premises: (1) the need to assist and rebuild Japan as an American partner in the Pacific, which had become an American ocean after the second world war; (2) the need to aid and show commitment to Western Europe, especially France; (3) the need to save the southern half of the world from the "evils" of monolithic communism; and (4) the need to contain China. Yet in the 1960's (especially following the Sino-Soviet split) it became evident that these premises were irrelevant, if not ridiculous—especially in the face of a world cultural revolution, the rising demands

[6] Bernard Groslier and Jacques Arthaud, *Angkor* (New York, 1969), p. 11.

of youth everywhere for a new humanism, for participatory democracy and relevant education, for idealism and not ideology. But a new sub-story, that of "containment of communism," had already developed in this country. Despite an elective system of government, American politicians, even the most sensitive, became prisoners of that sub-story which interest groups exploited and related it to the larger American stories: freedom, democracy, free enterprise, fear of God. . . .

The problem here is not to agree with Michael Novak—that is easy—but rather to find or devise a mechanism through which knowledge of other countries' stories could influence American policy-makers as they form and define the substance of "national interest." If the need is particularly urgent for the United States because of its size and its power, it is also necessary for other countries to know the American stories—the American Dream, the distortions and mutilations of that Dream by the internal development of the American economic system, of politics, of the peculiar American culture, or the non-existence of one. It is tempting to say the obvious thing: only education can provide that mechanism. But what kind of education?

I do not claim to know the answer to this question. But I will state that the type of education I have in mind is of the sort that must be national enough for Americans to know their own stories and sub-stories and international enough for them to be aware of other human communities' stories. A survey by the *New York Times* (June 8, 1970) disclosed that "there is no scholar in the U.S. who devotes a major portion of his time to studying current affairs in North Vietnam, and there is no scholar specializing in Vietnamese studies with a tenured professorship at any American university"—and this despite a decade of costly U.S. involvement and intervention in Vietnam and the lives of her people. According to the same study, only six schools offer courses in the Vietnamese language; only one school in the country, Yale, offers Cambodian, and last semester only two students were enrolled in the course. Perhaps, as Michael Novak advises, at this stage it would be "wise not to act, or not to act too decisively." But again, what can be done when policy is already adopted, soldiers are marching, and bombs are dropping?

Above all national stories and sub-stories—American and Vietnamese, Chinese and Russian—there exists the often tragic but consistently moving story of Man, his strength and his weakness, his longing for eternity while grounded in a tormented life on earth. That majestic story also needs to be known. When the Vietnamese or the Laotians take their guns to fight against the American soldiers in humid jungles, when the youth in Europe or Japan attack the U.S. embassies, when the young Americans march in Washington, they are demanding that America translate into deeds, not words, the American story symbolized in the Declaration of Independence. The requirement then is humanism, which in Vietnamese and Chinese is *Nhan Ban* (the foundation of man). Within that humanism, Michael Novak's idea can bloom into 126 flowers—126 being the number of the present U.N. membership.

LOGIC AND STORY IN POLITICAL ACTION

David Little

Michael Novak argues that the "category 'story' illumines certain realities of practical politics and clarifies certain issues in political theory." In making his case, he appears to hold two things: (a) that the term "story" suggests a consistent, distinguishable method for describing "the logic of political action"; (b) that the implied method is appropriate, and probably preferable to other methods, for uncovering the sources of mistakes in political policies (e.g., U.S. policy in Vietnam), and for indicating a way to avoid mistakes in the future. Accordingly, Novak implies that his "method" is useful as a descriptive as well as an evaluative tool. I shall try to show that Novak claims too much for his approach, both as an analytic and as an evaluative device. Not that his proposal is altogether useless. Here and there he emphasizes worthwhile things, but he does not need his "method" to emphasize them.

In general, his proposal suffers from two disabilities: first, it confuses reflection on the "logic of political action," which is what he claims to be clarifying; second, it obscures certain unavoidable considerations which apparently must be taken into account in determining and justifying policy. We need to dispel these difficulties before we can appropriate what is helpful in this essay.

First, if Novak means for his account of the logic of political action to help us understand the way people justify political policies, he does not succeed. It is clear that to justify actions of any sort involves appealing to higher and more general principles and then, finally, to something like Novak's "sense of reality" or view of "the nature of things" in order to vindicate the principles of one's action. That is well and good, though from the point of view of understanding the logic of political action it is a mere beginning. Novak gets off the track by the way he introduces those slippery words "story" and "symbol." I do not mean these words could not be investigated to illuminate political discourse. I believe they can and we ought to attend to them. It is just that Novak has not helpfully scrutinized them.

To begin with, it is not clear how "symbol" and "story" function "logically" (Novak's word) in justifying political action. Symbols may *convey* the meaning of certain principles or of a particular sense of reality. Often a symbol, such as the flag, will, as Novak says, evoke an emotional response and thereby quicken action. However, the flag stands for or points to "what a country is all about"—namely the principles of its life. It does not make much sense to say that the principles of the American way of life "take their meaning" from the flag, or that the flag "defines" the meaning of those principles, as Novak's discussion and diagram on page 16 suggest.

Nor does "story" function in any distinctive or consistent way in Novak's account. Whereas "story" is supposed to constitute one "level of meaning" in his schema, it actually operates, in a most confusing way, on all five "levels." According to Novak, a "story" (a) orders actions; (b) gives "concrete shape to principles"; (c) "links symbols"; (d) provides a context of meaning for past, present and future actions; (e) "expresses the form of action and the temporal dimension of the sense of reality." These uses of "story" do not necessarily come to the same thing, because "story" is a very imprecise term. All it really means is an account or narrative. As is obvious from Novak's ambiguous treatment, a nation, such as the United States, could have *many* stories at the same time, and some of them could conflict with each other. A story of American political actions could conflict with the story of its principles ("deeds versus creeds"), one story of its principles might conflict with another, or the dominant sense of reality might conflict with the account of what its symbols stand for, and so on. In order to help us understand how "story" illuminates the logic of political action, Novak's method needs considerable straightening out.

Even more, it needs straightening out because of the confusing and arbitrary way Novak opposes "story" to "principles" (see pp. 19-20). He feels that principles are abstractions which, as such, are "coercive and disruptive of the concrete tissue of life." "Story" better captures, he believes, the fact that principles are always embodied in the concrete historical expressions of a nation's life. These expressions are particular and limited to the country's experience, and a people ought not to forget that. To disregard its "story"—as the Americans do at their worst—is to ignore the particularity of principles and to fancy them to be "universal" and readily applicable to all peoples. According to Novak, such selective attention to principles, and such pretension that they are universalizable, belies a "rationalistic" sense of reality, one more at home with abstractions than with concrete, living experience.

But, granting that Americans during their history have emphasized and at times tried to implement universal principles, how far does it carry us to admit that this fact is part of the American story? To become aware that the mission of America, and all the images and symbols expressive of that mission, is an indelible aspect of American experience hardly settles the matter of whether or in what way it is *good* for Americans to have a mission to the world. One may not like that part of the story; one may blame the poor Puritans for generating the idea in the first place, as Novak does by his hasty and invidious references to the Protestant story; one may think America ought to mind its own business, and thereby try to live down an important part of its story. But if that is a person's viewpoint, then he is responsible for giving reasons for it. By taking that position, he is inviting an argument over the substance and applicability of American principles in which he will have to try to defend his interpretation against others. In the process, he may, of course, be pushed (as many Americans are these days) to try to vindicate a particular interpretation according to a sense of reality he finds plausible. It seems to me that today we are precisely in the position of having to justify afresh the principles of American political action, and we urgently need clarification of the debate. Alas, we do not get that clarification from Novak's method. Undoubtedly, we will want to remember the "stories" of how, as a nation, we have concretely implemented and expressed our principles at home and abroad. But once we have done that, the debate is hardly over. We still have the problem of *which* story we favor according to *what* sorts of argument.

Novak has it in for principles but I don't understand why. When, on page 19, for example, he defines those functions of "story" which distinguish it, for some unknown reason, as a political category, he describes part of what we normally mean by a practical principle—something that gives meaning to present action and guidance for the future. Moreover, when he offers his first proposal (p. 24 ff.), it looks to me as though he is providing us with a principle of some sort. The point is that one cannot settle arguments by invoking "story" over against principle, even if it were clear what was being said. One properly settles arguments, if at all, by addressing particular claims and the reasons given for those claims.

If Americans have not been duly modest or respectful in dealing with the Vietnamese, which I take to be one practical conclusion of Novak's essay, there are various grounds on which Americans could be criticized, none of which requires invoking Novak's category "story." It might be argued, as it has been, that not to take the opinions, ways of doing things, and "sense of reality" of the Vietnamese into account is self-defeating from an American as well as from a Vietnamese point of view. It has long since become a cliché in the debate over Vietnam that the only way for the U.S. to have even a hope of succeeding is to train Americans in the language, thought forms, cultural outlook, etc. of the Vietnamese. It is, of course, very useful to reflect on why Americans have been so slow to take this obvious advice. But that is to reflect on why Americans are given to working against themselves; to reflect not on why they are so rational, but why, in this case, they are so *ir*rational with respect to achieving the ends they seek. Undoubtedly, Americans have been so unsuccessful in Vietnam partly because they have misapplied methods from one culture to another, as Novak says. But one does not need the category "story" to learn that.

There are still other grounds for criticizing Americans over their lack of respect for others, grounds that inhere in American principles themselves. "Making the world safe for diversity," the "right of self-determination," and the like are highly ambiguous principles, even as Americans have historically uttered and tried to implement them. These principles have, it is true, often been interpreted according to what *Americans* define as proper diversity or proper self-determination. But the principles have also been interpreted, often by the tradition of liberal disillusionment, in favor of respecting the rights of others to run their own affairs and cooperate with Americans as those others see fit.

Just what those principles shall mean in particular cases is open to conflicting interpretation, but clearly they can be interpreted so as to emphasize the obligations of the United States to restrain itself and to honor the "stories" of other peoples. If various individuals believe the United States has not lived up to those obligations, it is not necessary to depart from traditional American principles to make that case. It is simply necessary to argue that in given instances, and for specified reasons, American principles place much more stringent restraint on U.S. intervention than has been observed in practice.

I do not discount other possible grounds on which the U.S. could be criticized for lack of respect. Someone certainly might try appealing to a sense of reality different from the one that allegedly underlies the traditional principles of American life. That would be still another sort of argument, distinct from the ones I have already outlined, and it would be important to chart the particular ways it is distinct. But I need not go into that, for I think I have shown that it is possible to conceive of arguments that come to practical conclusions very similar to Novak's without confusing the discussion by invoking his method based on the category "story."

I conclude, then, that analyzing the logic of political action is an extremely delicate chore, and needs the sharpest intellectual tools we can devise. Novak does not give us those tools, though he has put terms like "story" and "symbol" on our agenda for further examination.

Second, I cannot see how Novak's method provides guidance for evaluating American foreign policy. When, on page 26, Novak comes to his second proposal—regarding mutual story-telling among nations—it seems to me that a certain evaluative framework for considering international conduct and political morality is simply assumed. As Novak applies the term "story," he appears to have built in the following restriction: "National stories are proper to the extent they recognize their limitations, to the extent, that is, that they respect the rights of other nations to tell their stories and act upon them as they see fit." Such a "principle" clearly lies behind his strictures against U.S. policy in Vietnam. Presumably not any national story—such as the one the Nazis told—would be considered proper or acceptable if it infringed this restriction. But if that is what Novak is arguing, then he is assuming the principle broadly known as the "right of self-determination," and he is responsible to defend it, and to show how it can and should guide policy-makers faced with intervening or not intervening in one way or another. His notion "story" desperately begs the moral premise in his argument.

This is a particularly poignant problem in the light of Novak's admission that the United States is a "planetary power," and therefore "interventionist" simply by having the size and power it does. Surely, to take that fact seriously is to grant that part of the United States' "story" is its own unavoidable universal impact. And to admit America's impact is to invite the regulation of its power and influence according to some principles that define the moral responsibilities of all who share in the "planetary story." Whether these responsibilities be defined according to the traditional American creed and its various forms of expression, or whether they shall be defined by some other content, is, it seems to me, very much open to question and debate. Similarly, whether there is or is not "one form of human reason" which can provide men with some common presuppositions for moral reflection is also very much open to question and investigation. Abrupt assertions about these matters, such as Novak makes on pages 49-50, are not enlightening.

Novak gives the impression that his method enables him to avoid the hard, involved, evaluative questions regarding U.S. intervention in Vietnam that I and others have attempted to sort out. I, along with many critics of U.S. policy in Vietnam, am charged with imposing a "logical structure" on the debate that sees things only in terms of "principle and fact," but does not see the more important matters of symbol, story and sense of reality that are supposed to lie behind the discussion. This conceptual short-sightedness purportedly blinds me and others to what is really the problem with U.S. policy in Vietnam, namely, the lack of appreciation and respect for the Vietnamese and their story.

Novak is unpersuasive, though not because he unfairly charges that in thinking about the war I, and others, may not have taken sufficient account of the Vietnamese sense of reality and way of life. That is always a possibility, though one I have been aware of for some time. Novak is unpersuasive because, even within my frame of mind, I can understand and appreciate all of his illustrations regarding the "culture gap" between American and Vietnamese practices. For example, I do not need the category "story" to show me that the behavior of some American servicemen is as absurd and inappropriate as it appears to Novak.

Moreover, I am not persuaded that Novak is able to avoid the basic evaluative frame of reference with which I and many others have approached the war. The fundamental problem for me has always been whether there were any "good reasons" at all for U.S. military intervention in Vietnam, particularly in 1965. I am gratified that Novak thinks, as I do, that on balance there were sound reasons to believe at that time that U.S. intervention "could have played a role in Vietnamese history which the Vietnamese themselves might have appreciated in their own terms." What is more, I agree with him that once the intervention had taken place the United States had assumed responsibilities such that it could not "morally withdraw

. . . without tending first to the military, political, economic and cultural ill-effects a precipitate withdrawal might have."

Further, I am compelled to agree with Novak (and with others who make the same point without the benefit of the notion "story"), that many of the *means* employed by the United States have been indiscriminate and disproportionate in relation to the ends sought. I hereby confess that in *American Foreign Policy and Moral Rhetoric* I did not devote enough space to evaluating and criticizing U.S. military strategy and tactics from a moral point of view. Of course, I was not totally silent on the subject, and I did, after all, supply Novak with some of his most telling references against the use of indiscriminate means (e.g., the quotation from Robert Thompson, at fn. 18)!

Even within my frame of mind, it is possible to argue that when the U.S. Government has asserted, as it has on occasion, that a policy involving reliance on "mini-brute force" is "necessary" or "unavoidable," or that the use of defoliants and the like have no harmful long-range effects on the environment, the Government is making claims that are clearly testable and subject to criticism. I believe we now have a good deal of persuasive evidence that these particular claims, at least, were in great measure false, and for that reason alone are liable to moral censure. (However, all that seems to follow from such a conclusion is that the U.S. ought to stop using those particular means, as there is some evidence that it is beginning to do. Agitation directed specifically at altering the use of such means has been strangely uninteresting to many critics of the war.)

The main point is that when it gets down to moral evaluation of the war, Novak has not shown that he can escape thinking in relation to just-war criteria regarding the ends and means of the use of violence. (He himself refers to the criteria off-handedly on page 39.) Until there is reason to believe otherwise, it is according to these evaluative criteria that one must try to assess whether there were any good reasons for military intervention in the first place, as well as whether the manner in which the intervention was executed can be justified. If we admit that, then we must also admit that when we morally evaluate the war, we have decidedly *not* avoided the realm of principle and fact.

Naturally, I do not mean to imply from this that the task of assessment according to just-war principles is cut and dried. The issues are extremely complex. Moreover, I have not the slightest doubt that Novak's intuitions about the subtle relevance of symbol, image and attitude to moral evaluation are important. I can even conceive that because of a certain sense of reality that, say, the Vietnamese have, some of the just-war categories need to be applied in ways drastically different from the traditional Western ways, or, possibly, that several of the categories are, in fact, not applicable. *But we have to be shown, with care and in detail, that that is the case.* If Novak had undertaken to do this task, he would have performed an invaluable service. He might then have shown specifically how to go about determining the way "symbolic experience" affects the realm of "principle and fact," rather than asserting, in a very peculiar manner, the *a priori* superiority of one over the other.

Interestingly enough, the just-war categories make allowance for the very right to respect that, when all is said and done, Novak is at pains to ensure. The whole point of just-war doctrine is to provide criteria for determining legitimate political self-defense. In other words, the right to self-defense presupposes "a people with a story"—if one wants to put it that way—a people who have a right to tell that story and to act upon it, free of arbitrary interference. Whether or not such conditions exist in South Vietnam, as well as in Laos and Cambodia, is, of course, what the continuing debate is about. But without trying to settle that complicated question here, nothing in Novak's essay demonstrates that just-war principles are irrelevant, or that his method does not presuppose them. On the contrary, his method seems to beg extensive and precise discussion of just these principles.

Incidentally, on the basis of the material I have consulted on Vietnam, and especially John McAlister's *Vietnam: The Origins of Revolution* (which Novak does not cite), I am inclined to think that the "story" of the Vietnamese themselves is a good deal more complex and involved than Novak allows. According to McAlister, the "revolutionary nationalism" in Vietnam was essentially a Western import. The values of mobility, political participation, achievement and so on, were held out to the Vietnamese by the French with one hand, and denied to them with the other. The result was a revolutionary situation upon which the northern Communists capitalized. While this "revolutionary ethos" is clearly at odds with much of the traditionalist peasant culture referred to by Novak, the relevant "stories" are very mixed indeed. As with the "American story," so analysis of the Vietnamese story invites much more refinement than Novak offers.

Michael Novak's essay properly reminds us of two things:

one, that we need to turn our attention to the logic of political action; and, the other, that images, symbols, attitudes, and even "stories," if we can make the notion clear, play an important role in political action. But so far as advancing our understanding of these matters, I am afraid Novak's attempt must be regarded as a false start.

REALEPISTEMOLOGIE CONFRONTS REALPOLITIK

Daniel C. Maguire

The Government fashions an imaginary world that pleases it, and then comes to believe in the reality of that world and acts as though it were real.
—Hans J. Morgenthau, *The New York Times Magazine* (April 18, 1965)

Michael Novak wants to know how policy-makers know, and his concern is a wise one, threatening only to fools. His subject, a disastrously neglected one, is the epistemology of politics. His passion is realism. *Realepistemologie* confronts *realpolitik*. Novak illuminates his point by examples drawn from the American intervention in Vietnam. That complex intervention, though it is defended by no one as a masterpiece of statecraft, does provide choice opportunities for the study of the knowing processes that brought it about. But the problem of "knowing" that Novak addresses affects more things than Vietnam. I shall approach the problem on a somewhat broader base and shall use other examples. I will employ the category "myth" as my basic epistemological unit.

Words are like people: they have many relatives and companions. When you decide to marry a word to your particular purpose, it is thus well to make clear in advance that it is the word you want and not the whole family of associations. "Myth," of course, is a much used and therefore well-battered word. In spite of its varied usage, "myth" remains in linguistic currency, and, if carefully defined, can be serviceable.

Myth, in my usage, is this: it is a complex of feelings, attitudes, symbols, memories, and experienced relationships through which reality is refracted, filtered, and interpreted. That, admittedly, is a mouthful, so let me justify it by suggesting where myth, thus defined, fits into the processes of man's knowing.

It is a dangerous fallacy to think of the mind as a docile camera or mirror that passively and accurately reflects things back to us as they are. Human perception is active and not just receptive. That which is becoming known is related to the already known. We know in the same way that we define, by relating one thing to another. Relating one thing to others is not something that we do after we come to know the thing in isolation. Relating is essential to the knowing process; we know by relating.

It makes sense, then, to say that knowing is relational and dynamic. When an object becomes known it is brought into a community of other knowns, to be set in a meaning-giving, already familiar context. The experience of meaning derives from seeing things as fitting into and relating to the overall universe of our knowledge. Even if something new is known, it is given meaning and it makes sense only when we see that it somehow relates to the already known. Otherwise the new item is like the proverbial man from Mars, meaningless and disturbing.

All of this may seem unforgivably pedantic and unnecessary, so I must be quick to relate it to myth and down-to-earth politics. Indeed, the major part of my remarks will be directed to showing examples of myth in concrete situations.

Myth is one mental mechanism that serves to give meaning. Meaning is to the mind what oxygen is to the lungs and food is to the body. Whatever serves to give us the experiences of meaning is valuable, and so myth is valuable. We are all equipped by our experience with countless myths. New experiences and data are fed into our operative myths and thus acquire relationship and meaning. This is not to say that the experience of meaning achieved by way of myth is necessarily objective or true. A myth may give us a fallacious experience of meaning by relating a new experience to irrelevant attitudes, symbols, memories, and stories.

For example, the feminists in our midst are belatedly reminding us that the notion of woman (in both male and female heads) is heavily *mythed*. The myths of womanhood to which we are heir tell us that woman is essentially a creature of "die Küche, die Kirche, und die Kinder"; that these are the realities that identify the woman properly; that when these realities engage her she is most perfectly revealed in her true meaning as a person. If she is doing something else like becoming a surgeon, or a politician, or an astronaut, we may indeed applaud her feat, but, thinking through the myth, we know that she is doing these things "even though" she is a woman. The "even though" is not going to be explicit, especially in these days, but an honest scrutiny of our unspoken consciousness would show that the "even though" is there. (If any man doubts the presence of "die Küche" myth of womanhood in himself, let him ask how he would feel if the

President, all of his Cabinet, and 98 per cent of his Congress were women instead of men! To most honest men, the thought is unthinkable. The myths will not permit it. After all, it was only a few years ago that the myths even permitted women to vote.)

The "Küche" myth derives from many factors in our cultural history. Indeed, for a long time, the myth may have been a good myth that truly characterized the best possibilities of woman in a certain milieu. It may have represented the only way to apportion roles and understand one's nature in particular social contexts. Maybe. But now the realization is growing bright that the context has changed and the myths have not. The real, existent possibilities of woman are not now appreciated directly but are viewed, rather, through the filter of old myths. Hence the furor of women who refuse to accept the child-filled kitchen as their natural habitat and the symbol of their being.

The "Küche" myth illustrates some of the important characteristics of myths in general. Myths are stubborn. They are deep-rooted and strong. No wonder the feminists are shrill! Data which does not fit the view enshrined in the myth is simply expelled. The experience of many generations of educated women functioning professionally has not dissipated the prevailing myths of womanhood. "Die Küche" myth also illustrates, quite importantly, that myths can be wrong even when well grounded in history and widely held.

But myths can also be good and true and helpful. Take the myth of "the good old American know-how." "The difficult we do immediately, the impossible takes a little longer," goes the rhetoric of the myth. There is no small grounding for this myth, given the variety of American exploits in technology and in attempts at democracy.

A lot of good has derived from this myth. In various fields of technology, Americans have enjoyed some signal successes. Often their confidence was not suggested by the manifest data of the situation but rather by the myth, which buoyed them and carried them to success. It is to be remembered, however, that the "American know-how" myth has been less felicitous in foreign policy decisions where sensitivity to the foreign situation was needed and not the myths of the American psyche. This myth also illustrates that the same myth can be helpful or unhelpful depending on the context.

Let us turn now to myths in action in the political arena. Wartime is very mythogenetic and illustrates in an extreme form how myth can dominate individual and social cognition. Take the Spanish-American War. The causes regularly cited for this war are the extreme harshness of Spain's Cuban policy, the leaked and published letter of the Spanish minister in Washington that insulted President McKinley, and the sinking of the Maine with the attendant loss of 266 American lives. These causes do not give an adequate explanation of the consequent military outburst. A new government had just come to power in Spain that appeared to be more moderate in its attitude toward Cuba; the imprudent minister was immediately removed with proper apologies; and, as George Kennan says of the *Maine*:

> . . . there has never been any evidence that the Spanish government had anything to do with the sinking of the vessel. . . . Spanish authorities, as well as our own consul-general in Havana, had begged us not to send the vessel

there at that time for the very reason that they were afraid this might lead to trouble. The Spanish government did everything in its power to mitigate the effects of the catastrophe, welcomed investigation, and eventually offered to submit the whole question of responsibility to international arbitration—an offer we never accepted.[1]

Possibilities of fruitful negotiations with Spain were ignored. Alternatives to war were bypassed. Demonological myths about the Spanish and romantic martial myths obsessed the popular consciousness. Myth-based hysteria prevailed in the press, the populace, and the Congress. Expansionist myths were also at work, and before long the Philippines were seized and put under the American flag. A "hard-nosed," rational realist explanation of this whole adventure which ignored the operation of myth would fail. It would be unrealistic to ignore the myths that affected national cognition in that hysterical moment. As Milton Mayer says: "Hysterical peoples—like hysterical persons—may not be expected to know that they are hysterical."[2] Neither are persons or peoples in the grips of distorting myths likely to diagnose their own condition. Too often it is only fierce tragedy that ultimately jars a mind free of its baneful myths.

World War I serves to illustrate how new myths can succeed old myths in such wise that the mythic influence allows persons to be totally unaware of the sudden inconsistency and discontinuity in their outlook and behavior. At the time the war was erupting, Americans were safely ensconced in the myths

[1] *American Diplomacy, 1900-1950* (New York and Toronto, 1951), p. 14.

[2] *On Liberty: Man v. The State* (Santa Barbara, Calif., 1969), p. 123.

of idealistic isolation. Wilson was re-elected on the grounds that "He kept us out of war." But when events unsettled our neutralist stance, a whole new mythology came to be: The world was to be made safe for democracy. (It might have been said, with greater accuracy, that the world was to be made safe for shipping, but American martial myths are mystical in tone and we do not stoop to the pragma of mere and mortal nations.)

In this same period, the reality of the German people was filtered through new myths. The Germans—who had been rather admired for their industry and skill in science—became Huns; the German language became taboo; sauerkraut had to be renamed "liberty cabbage." And religion animated many of the war myths, as it tends always to do in times of any great crisis. Revealing are the words of the Bishop of London: "As I have said a thousand times, I look upon it as a war for purity, I look upon everyone who dies in it as a martyr."[3] The madness of much of this is apparent to those not gripped in the myths of that day. At the time, however, all the moves seemed to the movers to be the product of tough and practical realism. Indeed, the sanctimonious approach to foreign policy that is typically American demands that it be defensively draped in the regalia of realism. That we are realists in our wars is a popular and untrue myth. (Novak says that Vietnam was a realists' war. I disagree. The realists have not yet had their war.)

The psychiatrist, Jerome Frank, has taken much interest in the psychology of international hostility. He tells of a

[3] Cited by Roland Bainton in *Christian Attitudes Toward War and Peace* (New York and Nashville, 1960), p. 207.

Russian-speaking American psychologist who visited Russia in 1960 and interviewed a large number of people. Most of those interviewed felt that the American Government deludes and exploits its people and is not fully supported by them. They felt that American leaders could not be trusted and that their foreign policy borders on madness.

Parallel interviews in America and in Russia showed that almost 100 per cent of those contacted felt that the national goal of the other nation is domination or expansion and that the nuclear plans of the other nation call for a pre-emptive first strike. Each nation sees its own motives in offering foreign aid as altruistic and the intentions of the other nation as predatory.[4]

Frank's description of the characterization of the enemy in time of hostility squares with my usage "myth." It further illustrates the presence of irrational and unobjective mental mechanisms in the processes of social cognition. He writes at one point:

> In 1942 and again in 1966 respondents were asked to choose from a list of adjectives those that best described the people of Russia, Germany, and Japan. In 1942 the first five adjectives chosen to characterize both Germans and Japanese [enemies] included warlike, treacherous, and cruel, none of which appeared among the first five describing the Russians [allies]; in 1966 all three had disappeared from American characterizations of the Germans and Japanese

[4] *Sanity and Survival: Psychological Aspects of War and Peace* (New York, 1968), pp. 117-118. Frank's reference here is to U. Bronfenbrenner, "The Mirror Image in Soviet-American Relations: A Social Psychologist's Report," *Journal of Social Issues,* 17 (1961), p. 46.

[allies] but now the Russians . . . were warlike and treacherous.[5]

J. Glenn Gray has written the best phenomenological study on the psychology of military man known to this writer: *The Warriors,* subtitled Reflections on Men in Battle. This volume offers more relevance than the title would seem to promise, especially since our psychosphere is still generously militaristic. A militaristic worldview is not confined to the military but is very much a part of our political and social psychology. Modern man, for all his irenic dreams, is still *homo bellicus.*

Gray cites the totalitarian and abstract nature of the modern warrior. Today, there is none of the old professional soldier's respect for the enemy as the able opponent, but neither is the enemy viewed as a kind of a sub-human animal. Rather, Gray says, "our wars are becoming ever more totalitarian in character. Increasingly, we cannot fight without an image of the enemy as totally evil, for whom any mercy or sympathy is incongruous, if not traitorous."[6] "The image [of the enemy] is abstract to a degree hardly equaled in other images because it refuses to see any quality of the foe except his ideology."[7] The modern warrior "is not fighting men but embodiments of undifferentiated evil."[8]

5 *Ibid.,* p. 134.

6 *The Warriors* (New York, 1967), p. 146. The book was first published in 1959 by Harcourt, Brace and Company and was little noticed at first. Gradually it began to attract attention and was published by Harper as a Torchbook with an introduction by Hannah Arendt.

7 *Ibid.,* p. 154.

8 *Ibid.,* p. 140.

Gray attributes the totalitarian abstractness of the modern military mind partly to the need for a short-cut to meaning in the complex and ideologized conflicts of this time. "We strive to keep an equilibrium amid a thousand impressions and to make sense of our world by elimination when it becomes impossible to do so by synthesis."[9] "Experience is confirmatory and no longer exploratory. Only that part of it is digested which accords with the soldier's grasp of reality."[10] This describes well the stubborn imperviousness of the myth-bound mind to new and corrective information.

It would be a mistake to feel that only the masses are prey to perverting myths. Prestige and high office lend no immunity. Recall the response of the United States Supreme Court in the *Korematsu* case. Korematsu was one of the 112,000 Japanese-Americans who were quite literally corralled in 1942, kept in stables and stalls far from their West Coast homes, on order of the Western Command of the Army of the United States. These persons were imprisoned without charges or due process simply because they were part of "an enemy race." The Supreme Court majority ruled that they could not "reject as unfounded the judgment of the military authorities." Explain that, if you would, without the category of myth or story.

The Presidents of the United States have in recent decades been riding on popular myths that have only lately begun to rattle. The myths that grace the presidential office are both royal and religious in quality. The inauguration of a President is always an event in the history of piety, and the awe that is accorded the incumbent says everything but *"vive le roi!"*

[9] *Ibid.*, p. 133.

[10] *Ibid.*, p. 155.

The President is not nearly so circumscribed in his powers as is, for example, the Prime Minister of England. The advantage of England, of course, is that it has acknowledged its need for regality. It has kept the throne but severed it from power. In the United States, executive power has significantly royal flavorings. It lacks the royal signs but has much of the thing they signify.

The swollen independence of the presidency has been supported by the martial myths that naturally accrue to the title of Commander-in-Chief in an age of chronic war and preparation for war. Tocqueville, in his *Democracy in America,* wrote that war in democratic nations

> must invariably and immeasurably increase the powers of civil government; it must almost compulsorily concentrate the direction of all men and the management of all things in the hands of administration. If it lead not to despotism by sudden violence, it prepares men for it more gently by their habits.[11]

War and supposed danger do induce a thrust toward more central power. National threat also stirs the "Il Duce" myth that is never too deeply buried in our still quite primitive breasts. For over thirty years, the United States has lived with threat. Executive power has heightened and it has broad popular support. The wide support for the Cambodian invasion shows this, as does the endless patience of citizens with the expensive excesses of the Department of Defense. Such support does not derive from constitutional expertise or debate on the balance of powers, but is largely unreflective and mythic

11 Alexis de Tocqueville, *Democracy in America* (London and New York, 1900), vol. II, p. 282.

in its roots. There is no reason to suppose that it would not also support a decision of the President as Commander-in-Chief to use nuclear weapons to protect American lives. We are not all that far from antiquity, where resistance to the leader was a sin of impiety.

But, happily, the myths of the royal American presidency are hurting a bit. Two incidents, which are apparently unrelated but are actually the yield of the same myth, reveal this: in both Cambodia and in his attempt to put royal dress on the White House guard, President Nixon has had to withdraw. These two exploits were too candidly royal for many of the President's subjects. That is encouraging, but, still, the citizenry are not yet ready even to consider, for example, something that the founding fathers very carefully considered—the advantages of a plural executive over a single president. There are, however, harbingers of maturity abroad in the land. The harbingers, unfortunately, are rather late and not obviously sufficient. The qualitative change in weaponry, among other things, has produced a qualitative change in governmental power. Power is still being wielded under the old and now inadequate rubrics. The myths have not as yet permitted us to confront this most radical structural problem of our society. The detection of operative myths in what Jacques Ellul calls "our psychopolitical universe"[12] is thus not just a beguiling donnish pasttime. Survival and the humanization of the species are also at issue. Myths are serious.

With mercy toward all readers, I will limit myself to one

[12] Cf. Jacques Ellul, *The Political Illusion* (New York, 1967). This work is a powerful discussion of the illusions of *homo politicus*. Ellul argues the political irrelevance of facts that do not fit into our symbolic schemes of understanding.

more example of myth in action. I refer to a classic in political mythology: President Johnson's speech at Johns Hopkins University in 1965.[13] The Crusade in Vietnam was young when this speech was given; the President had only to defend the deaths of 400 Americans. But the myths were present in full flower in this influential and revealing address, and they support my contention that even Vietnam has not been a realist's war. Here the realities of Vietnam were being filtered through the myths and stories generated in other times and places. As usual, the mythic interpretation smothered dissimilarities and false historical analogies:

> This is the principle [freedom] for which our ancestors fought in the valleys of Pennsylvania.
>
> We must say in Southeast Asia as we did in Europe. . . .
>
> We have it [responsibility] for the same reason we have a responsibility for the defense of freedom in Europe.

The sanctimonious righteousness of America's messianic purpose is clear in the speech, even when one cannot hear the unctious tone of its delivery (cf. Novak's opening observations on the American self-image):

> We want nothing for ourselves.
>
> . . . we fight for principles, rather than territory or colonies.
>
> Our patience and determination are unending.
>
> . . . no nation need ever fear that we desire their land, or to impose our will, or to dictate their institutions.
>
> We are there because we have a promise to keep.

Somewhat discordantly, the President added: "We will do this because our own security is at stake." (At times, the myths, like the gods, collide with one another.)

[13] *Department of State Bulletin,* LII (April 26, 1965), pp. 606-610.

Our intentions are not just good but religiously blessed and motivated:

> . . . in the words of the Bible: "Hitherto shalt thou come, but no further."
>
> . . . it is our best and prayerful judgment . . . [concerning the need for bombing].
>
> We may well be living in the time foretold many years ago when it was said: "I call heaven and earth to record this day against you. . . ."

Wartime myths require a demonological caricature of the enemy, and Johnson pointed to "the deepening shadow of Communist China." The word "Communist," along with its antithetical counterpart "freedom," activate more myths than most words in our political lexicon. China has become the fullest embodiment of the undifferentiated evil of communism. Johnson noted gravely: "It is a nation which is helping the forces of violence in almost every continent." His myth-bound convictions here were not jarred by the fact that our war record in the past twenty years is unmatchable and that in that period we have sold or given away more than $50 billion in arms to other countries.[14] Myths repel unsuitable facts as a body repels a foreign substance.

In 1965, Hans Morgenthau warned about government's "tendency to conduct foreign and military policy not on their own merits, but as exercises in public relations."[15] This was

[14] Cf. Richard J. Barnet, *The Economy of Death* (New York, 1969), pp. 164-66.

[15] "We Are Deluding Ourselves in Vietnam," *New York Times Magazine* (April 18, 1965), reprinted in *Vietnam: History, Documents, and Opinions on a Major World Crisis*, ed. Marvin E. Gettleman (New York, 1965), p. 374.

written before Nixon and his administration, where the public relations concern is an obsession and a way of life. The Nixon Administration is skilled in the art of propaganda, to use a hoarier and more descriptive term. They have learned that if you tweak a few symbols in the consciousness of the body politic and evoke the appropriate myths, mass compliance is your reward. The evocative words are everywhere: bugging out, never lost a war, pride and honor, American lives, freedom, democracy, law and order. With the proper myths in the atmosphere, disagreeable facts will not register in any significant way. Conson Prison, My Lai, and the deaths of over 700,000 persons will scarcely make a blip on the popular psychic screen.

Because we were not fed by the German myths of the 1930's and early 1940's, we marvel at how good German folk could stomach the atrocities of their government. Not caught by Soviet myths, we wondered how good Russians could be so little affronted by Budapest and by Prague. People who do not share our myths are wondering at us.

Propaganda is powerful because it knows how to handle myths. If anything is more dangerous, it is the "realism" of analytical, reasonable men who abhor all this talk of story and myth and the untidiness such terms bring to policy discussions. No one is free of myths. They are part of our way of knowing. As we demythologize, we remythologize. Our only hope is reflection and a cultivated love for exposure to facts, especially threatening facts that disturb our schemes. But the man who thinks his reason is untrammeled by myth is a fool, and a dangerous one at that.

RELATIVISM, MORALITY, AND POLITICS

Theodore R. Weber

Although this paper by Michael Novak moves in and out of several theoretical and practical controversies, its principal concern is to change the methodology—and thereby improve the practice—of United States foreign policy. Novak's indictment is as follows: The United States often is politically unwise and morally bad in its use of national power in international politics. These faults are *characteristic,* and not merely random or accidental or the result of the moral and intellectual failures of particular policy-makers. They derive ultimately from a "sense of reality" and a national "story" which make us insensitive to the rich, human reality of other political actors, which predispose us to mistakes in political analysis, and equip us with misleading theories of political and moral behavior.

To correct these faults and counteract their tendencies, Dr. Novak makes two "modest proposals." One advocates expanding our consciousness and awareness to accept the relativity of the American "sense of reality" and to increase enormously our sensitivity to the real and full humanity of other peoples. The other advocates using the literary category "story" as an instrument of the foreign policy process.

There is nothing novel in the first proposal. It has been advanced on numerous occasions by other writers—most often, perhaps, by those "realists" who are so frequently attacked and as a rule so badly misrepresented in Novak's paper.[1] The call for transcendence and criticism of American parochialism and "innocence," for encounter with concreteness and particularity, for attention to non-rational and incalculable as well as rational and calculable factors, for appreciation of cultural subtlety and historical depth, for a more comprehensive reading of national interest—all this is familiar to anyone who knows the pertinent literature.[2] Novak could have con-

1 Novak packages together several types of realists, confuses and combines their brands of realism, and then attacks all of them for the same alleged faults. Some are realists of the type of Hans Morgenthau and George Kennan—men deeply sensitive to the range and variety of elements in international politics (and critics of U.S. policy in Vietnam). Others are "realistic" in the sense of being hard-headed, no-nonsense calculators, who read reality exclusively in material terms and treat all foreign policy decisions as problems of business administration. Yet others seem to be realists in the philosophical sense: their realism (advocacy of "universals") is set in contrast to the nominalistic emphasis on particularity. Novak's shuffling of varieties of realists helps to explain—but not to justify—his railing against a "realist's righteousness" and his charge that Vietnam is a "realist's war."

2 Reinhold Niebuhr has made all of these points many times over. Consider, for example, these words published in 1952: "We have had little experience in the claims and counter-claims of man's social existence, either domestically or internationally. We therefore do not know social existence as an encounter between life and life, or interest with interest in which moral and non-moral factors are curiously compounded. It is therefore a weakness of our foreign policy, particularly as our business community conceives it, that we move inconsistently from policies which would overcome animosities to us by the offer of economic assistance to policies which would destroy resistance by

tributed—and indeed should contribute—to work already done in this line by developing more fully what might be called an "aesthetic epistemology of political reality." That possibility is implicit in his paper and needs to be made explicit. Adequately done, it would demonstrate how aesthetic means of knowing can penetrate political existence with more apprehension and comprehension than is possible to other means. It would have to accomplish this while avoiding the dangers of irrationalism and excessive subjectivism to which romanticist epistemologies are inclined.

The second proposal, however, is the center of Novak's attention. He wants to demonstrate how the use of the category "story" can confer practical effectiveness and moral maturity on the conduct of United States foreign policy. My response, therefore, will deal primarily with that claim. First I want to make some comments on the category "story" itself.

I.

A literary category is the focus of this presentation, but the author is interested not in the literary properties of the story

the use of pure military might. We can understand the neat logic of either economic reciprocity or the show of pure power. But we are mystified by the endless complexites of human motives and the varied compounds of ethnic loyalties, cultural traditions, social hopes, envies and fears which enter into the policies of nations, and which lie at the foundation of their political cohesion.

"In our relations with Asia these inconsistencies are particularly baffling. We expect Asians to be grateful to us for such assistance as we have given them; and are hurt when we discover that Asians envy, rather than admire, our prosperity and regard us as imperialistic when we are 'by definition' a 'non imperialistic nation' " (*The Irony of American History* [New York, 1952], pp. 41-42).

but in the story as a politico-social fact. The creation of the story is art not for art's sake but for the people's sake. The telling and re-telling of the story is less for the purpose of provoking laughter or wonder or sadness than for shaping or arousing the memory and calling up an authoritative vision of the future. We are concerned, therefore, with the societal functions of the story. The story, as Novak represents it, functions in the following ways: (1) as an *organizing* principle, which brings order to human experience by linking symbols in a sequence of past, present and future; (2) as a *hermeneutical* principle, which interprets the meaning of (or confers meaning on) experience by locating it and analyzing it within a culturally provided framework; (3) as a *dynamic* principle, which has the power to "engender sequences of actions," i.e., to create the future out of the experienced present in the light of the remembered past; (4) as a *socializing* principle, which confers identity on a person through his acknowledgement of and sharing in the story of the group(s) of which he is a member. In all these ways the story manifests and actuates the concreteness of human, social and individual experience by expressing the sense of reality in the particularity of action, and by interpreting the particular action with reference to the sense of reality.

If I have represented Dr. Novak's understanding of "story" correctly, I have no quarrel with him on the general proposition that it is important—indeed, necessary—to the politically prudent and morally responsible conduct of foreign policy. The further questions of the manner and degree of its importance do provide—or seem to provide—the occasion for some argument, but I shall turn to those questions later. For the present, I should like to ask him to clarify and refine the category with reference to the following distinctions.

a. What is the relationship of "story" to "history"? May the story of a people be purely imaginary, or must it have some basis in events which actually transpired but which are remembered and repeated in "storied" fashion? If the latter is the case, what is the relationship between the remembered and interpreted form of past experience and "what actually happened"?[3] That is the basic question of historical method. It surfaces in Novak's paper—for example, in his recognition of the contrast between the self-serving story of American innocence and the accusing realities of slavery, racial segregation, expropriation and extermination of the American Indians, imperialism, and the like. But it is not carefully considered, and the distinction is clouded over when he allows "historical record" to substitute for "story," and when he distinguishes "report" from "story" by defining the former as "a description of an act or event" and the latter as the description of a "sequence of acts or events."[4]

The distinction between what is "storied" and what "occurred" becomes of critical importance when a people is confronted with an account of its activity which contradicts its "story," and when the contradictory account is supported

[3] Novak could pursue this question profitably with the aid of H. Richard Niebuhr's distinction between "internal history" and "external history" in *The Meaning of Revelation* (New York, 1941).

[4] This distinction between "report" and "story" is arbitrary. An event is such by reason of its location in a sequence, and a description at least intends to report and not to make subjective or confessional statements, whether its object be a single occurrence or several which appear to be related to each other.

too firmly by criteria of verification and a "cloud of witnesses" simply to be dismissed. Is it enough to say that in such a case the clash is between different senses of reality, and not between the true and the false? Is it necessary to convert from one sense of reality to another, or is it possible to revise the story and incorporate the new understandings into the fundamental symbolic pattern? If revision and incorporation are not possible, does the new history yield a new story—or only the conviction that all stories are false, that the linking of events always is arbitrary, that no promise of the future justifies the commitment of our loyalty and our lives?

b. What are the differences—and what are the political-moral consequences of the differences—between stories that take their framework and dynamic from history and those that take them from nature? Novak reveals his own reality bias by characterizing the story category as temporal thinking about temporal acting in international politics, which is—according to his view of reality—"an arena of constant change and constant interaction." Time and change, in this view, not only are real and important but may, in fact, be the only reality. Salvation of the present requires movement through time to the temporal past or temporal future as normative. The Vietnamese story, as he reports it, is otherwise: ". . . what is real has the quiet power and inner peace of ordered rice paddies, seasons, laws of growth." Time is both unreal and disruptive of the real. Order is found in the "natural rhythms," not in the unique and concrete historical ordering of past, present and future. The story is not a myth of history with an unrealized future but a "myth of eternal return" (Eliade). The significance of these differences for Vietnam and comparable societies must not be overlooked. The Marxist and technocratic "stories"—both of which are Western—are literally at war with the traditional nature-oriented Vietnamese story. To speak of Ho Chi Minh's having accommodated Marxism to a Vietnam with no proletariat is to miss the point that what basically is at issue betwen Marxism and Vietnam cannot be accommodated. Both Marxism and the "logic of modernization"—quite apart from the United States intervention—drag Vietnam into time and history despite the power of its traditional story. Perhaps the victory of the dynamic over the static can be accomplished with more subtle effectiveness by some approaches than by others, but there should be no doubt that the temporalizing and historicizing of a cosmo- or nature-oriented society is far more revolutionary than changes in the personnel of government or even in the basic institutions. And what will happen when the energies and the fundamental problems of meaning, which heretofore have been sublimated in the eternal "rhythms of nature," are transposed into the disjointed and malleable movements of history (where the end of the process can be disclosed and apprehended symbolically, but never realized in its fullness)?

c. What is the difference, if any, between "story" and "ideology"? Depending on the definition of ideology, there might be no difference. What I mean to ask, however, is whether the story has a social source in a particular class or other group within the society. Is the original and primary function of the story perhaps that of consolidating and defending the interests of that particular group against any challenge from other members of the society? If so, is it possible to struggle within the terms of the story to rearrange the basic structure and distribution of societal power, or does a struggle with such radical aims require the destruction of the protective story?

These distinctions pertinent to the "story" category should be clarified systematically, so that the category itself may become more serviceable to the purposes which Michael Novak has in mind.

II.

The "story," as we have noted, is recommended by the author as a device for conferring practical effectiveness and moral responsibility on the conduct of United States foreign policy. Let us, then, evaluate his methodological claims.

a. The story tells us "what is going on." As Professor H. Richard Niebuhr taught us, that is the proper question with which to begin any moral inquiry—including those that pertain to political responsibility.[5] What is sought is not a bare factual statement but an interpretation—a rendering of the meaning of events. If we know the meaning of the events we know what projective pattern they fit into, and therefore we may be able to anticipate what will happen next and how a response on our part will be received. In this connection, Dr. Novak certainly is correct in arguing for an increase in sensitivity to the cultural density of the political situation, and for knowledge of national "stories" as clues to the operational frameworks of interpretation.

But is the story the *key* to what is going on? Is it the one

[5] Niebuhr's ethic of responsibility is set forth in his *The Responsible Self* (New York, 1963).

trustworthy and indispensable principle of interpretation? We should distinguish two possible ways in which national stories might be related to political events. First, people explain the meanings of political events to themselves with reference to the symbols and sequences of their own stories. If the first possibility is all that Novak means to emphasize, he is doing nothing more than stressing one factor that influences political behavior. If he is contending for the second, he is advancing a theory of political behavior, i.e., a general explanation of why peoples do what they do when they are doing politics.

I would expect Novak to deny that he is proposing a theory of political behavior, because a theory, i.e., a generalized explanation, would be inconsistent with his insistence on total openness to the concrete particularity of peoples in live situations. If we assume in advance that a group acting politically is a troupe of actors engaged in dramatic self-representation, we may de-sensitize ourselves to the possibility that a different explanation is concretely more faithful to historical actuality. Nevertheless, Dr. Novak's argument for the story conveys the impression that he is indeed advocating a theory of political behavior, even though he never says so directly. Certainly his use of the phrase "logic of political action" to explain the inner connections of the "levels of political discourse" creates the impression that the act at the lower end of the scale is an articulation of the story.[6] His claim that the story "engenders sequences of actions" and "shapes future choices," implies that historical action is the acting out of the story. The impression appears to be confirmed when he asserts that all

[6] Compare Henry David Aiken's discussion of "The Levels of Moral Discourse" in *Reason and Conduct* (New York, 1962).

of the strategic and tactical questions of political action are contained within the category "story."

Now if Novak does mean to advocate this theory of political behavior, he must test it out and not merely assert it. Is the theory the best way to account for the data and their configurations and dynamics in the immediate case? Does the theory serve consistently to explain political behavior in all instances of this type? Is the theory demonstrably a better generalization than other theories, e.g., Hobbesian, Marxian, Freudian? Perhap a dramatic theory of political behavior would pass these and other pertinent tests. Perhaps not. If, on the other hand, he does not want to contend for a theory, he must admit that knowing the story of the people with whom the policy-maker is dealing is but one factor of variable importance for analyzing and interpreting a political situation.

When American policy analysts study Russian power plays, they should ask whether any of the operational Russian "stories" accounts for the action: pursuit of historic Russian (not Communist) foreign policy objectives, world revolution, Holy Russia with Moscow as the "Third Rome," pan-Slavism. But they also should test out hypotheses which are not derived from any of the stories: an up-dating of geopolitics pertinent to the world balance of power, struggle in the Kremlin, use of belligerence in foreign affairs to distract from failure of domestic policies, improvement of access to raw materials or of bargaining position in world trade, etc. Similarly, the United States should have informed itself of the Vietnamese "story" and other aspects of Vietnamese culture, but it also should have looked at the Vietnamese situation with a far better understanding of the dynamics of revolutionary struggle, the limits of even vastly superior firepower in supporting a government with little real authority (and little grounds for claiming any), the role of naval and air power in a jungle war, and the nature of insurgency and counterinsurgency warfare.

If it should be argued that the American policy-planner would filter all of these elements through the medium of his own sense of reality and story, I would agree—but would insist, nevertheless, that that is a different matter. In analyzing Vietnam, or any other particular situation, the planner should regard the "story" of the peoples involved as an important datum and principle of interpretation—but only as one of several factors to be considered in coming to understand the meaning, and therefore the policy implications, of the political situation.

b. Knowledge of the political role of stories and also of pertinent particular stories is necessary to the process of political communication.[7] What we say and write to others is transmitted not with a universal mathematical language which yields a single and univocal meaning, but with culture-drenched symbols which often translate into the universe of another culture a meaning quite different from the one intended. When we act politically we provide rhetoric to explain and justify our action, but the story expressed in the actions may be contradictory to the publicized account—or at least it may be read that way by others. It is true, then, that we must be sensitive to the role and substance of stories in order to know

[7] See, for example, the study of political communications between India and the United States in Harold D. Lasswell and Satish K. Arora, *Political Communication* (New York, 1969).

when and what we are communicating as well as how to communicate.

But such sensitivity does not confirm the moral responsibility of the communicative process. When, as a result of having learned the role of the story, we are wiser to the ways of communication we are not, therefore, necessarily more honest. Indeed, our increased wisdom may enable us to be more devious and deceptive with greater skill and success. We may recognize, of course, that such exploitation of the communicative process is imprudent, for it tends to destroy confidence in the credibility of our communications. But that points to a rule dictated by the nature of the relationships, and not by the story category as a political instrument. Or we may strive for honesty because honesty is virtue or because we take it as a duty or a responsibility to those with whom we deal. But such dispositions are implications of our own particular story, and again not of the story category as a political instrument.

We conclude, therefore, that in the area of political communication we may use the story to grow wiser and politically more skillful but we do not thereby necessarily become morally better.

c. Knowledge of stories discloses the substance of policy. Novak writes:

> *Before entering into a foreign policy commitment, American officials should answer these questions:* (1) *What is the story the United States wishes to tell in that part of the world?* (2) *What is the story the other nation in question wishes to tell?* (3) *What role can the United States best play in the story chosen by that other nation?* (4) *What role can the other nation play in the United States story?*

(5) *When conflicts in the stories arise, how are they to be resolved?*

Presumably the answers to those questions would define the policy. But in fact they cannot, for the formula as developed in this paper provides information but no criteria for judgment and decision The fifth question recognizes the need for such criteria, but Dr. Novak does not tell us how to resolve conflicts within the framework of the "story" method.

Consider, in this connection, questions #3 and #4—the "role definition" questions: If we determine what role we *can* play, does it follow that we *ought* to play it? Do other nations have the right to expect the United States to play foreign policy roles determined by their stories? Ought the United States to try to influence other countries to play roles prescribed by "our" story? Would that not be more of the "arrogance" of which we so often are accused? Does any nation have the right to expect other nations to play the role it sets for them?

What is Novak's view of the moral authority of the roles? The formula given above implies that they have none. Knowledge of the roles seems to have only pragmatic significance. "What role *can* the United States *best* play [italics mine] . . . ?" To know what role we can play best, and what roles we can play but not so well, and what roles we can play only poorly, is to be able to sort out the limiting and enabling factors which influence the formulation and conduct of policy. It is not, however, to know what we ought to do. In particular, it is not to know that we ought to play the role assigned to us in the other's story. But we cannot imagine that Novak means to assign only pragmatic significance to the roles and the knowledge of them. Historically developed and defined roles are part of the given of existence to which nations must accommodate themselves. "The overriding question," he writes, "is how persons from one national culture can come to understand people in other national cultures, in order to know what role to play in their history." The whole atmosphere of the paper suggests that we *should* (not only that we *can*) play the roles assigned in the stories. Therefore to know the role is to know that we ought to play that one and not another, and that sounds like a prescription for the content of foreign policy.

Should we, then, admonish the Israelis to accept the role assigned to them in the Egyptian story? Should the Czechs feel morally bound to accept their role in the story that is being acted out by Russian foreign policy? Should Castro have accepted for Cuba its traditional role in the United States story for the Caribbean? Should the United States act out the role which it is given in neo-Leninist interpretations of international politics? The answer to all these questions, I would assert, is "no." Stories, as they relate to international politics, serve the primary function of justifying the interests and programs of the groups that develop and promulgate them. With reference to the interests and programs of other groups, they reveal a range of factors which influence the prospects for inter-group relations, but they do not constitute a moral claim.

The conclusion would seem to throw us back to the first question as the prime determinant of policy: "What is the story that the United States wishes to tell in that part of the world?" I must confess to some bias against the phrasing of this question, because it sounds so typically American bourgeois. It is suggestive of preparations for a giant international advertising campaign, and reminiscent of admonitions to "counter communism" by "telling the story of the American way of life and free-enterprise capitalism." But those are not serious objections, and I certainly don't mean to imply that they express Novak's intention. The really serious problem is the role of the question in disclosing what our policy ought to be. It inquires about the story that we wish to tell through our policy, but does not ask why we should wish to tell it, or why we should prefer that particular American story to the several others that seem to be available. To answer questions like those we would have to go beyond the identification of stories to the declaration of value priorities and criteria for making fundamental choices. Of course, one might respond that the value priorities and criteria are contained in the fundamental American story, and that when the fundamental story is uncovered it should direct the course of United States foreign policy. However, in view of the many criticisms in his paper of what Novak portrays as the American story, it is hard to believe he would impose on the policy-maker the moral obligation to spell it out with American power in world affairs.[8] Perhaps what he really wants is a story that is not peculiarly "American," but that is developed from the concept if not the sociological reality of a community much more inclusive in its scope. At any rate, Dr. Novak has not shown us how the story as a method directs the determination of policy, as distinct from its role in providing useful informa-

[8] Two excellent historical studies of the "American story" are Russell B. Nye, *This Almost Chosen People* (Lansing, Mich., 1966), and Albert K. Weinberg, *Manifest Destiny* (Baltimore, 1935).

tion. It does not seem to give us the fundamental criteria for making judgments and decisions. It does not tell us how to choose among the several stories of one nation, or how to resolve conflicts between the stories of two or more nations.

In summary, the "story" is a useful but not sufficient instrument for foreign policy analysis, formulation, and implementation. It improves contextual analysis, but does not alone yield the meaning of political situations and events. It facilitates political communication, but does not tell us what to communicate or whether to be honest in our communicating. It uncovers important elements and conditioning factors of policy, but does not tell us what the policy ought to be. It makes policy more effective, but it does not create moral commitments to other factors in international politics.

Dr. Novak is making a good point, but he tends to oversell the story method on all of the above counts. *One* reason for the overselling is that he is so impressed—and rightly so—by the disastrous consequences of not learning and accommodating to the Vietnamese story that he tends to claim too much for the general utility and (note well) universal applicability of the story method, as well as for the moral authority of the stories themselves. *Another* reason is his tendency to assume that knowing (in the most comprehensive sense) is the way to political salvation. The great weight of his paper is on the urgency of improving our knowledge, awareness, understanding and sensitivity. When we come to know the peoples of other national cultures, we shall know what role to play in their story—and presumably we will play it. With a more mature and complete grasp of concrete reality we shall know what policies to prepare and how to execute them. However, that would be true only in an ordered and orderly universe, and for an anthropology which sees the basic problem of man in his historical particularity and not also in his egoism. The paper does not anticipate the possibility that wider vision and keener perceptiveness may show the divisions of international relations to be deeper and more inexorable than we have imagined, nor does it come to grips with the argument that both knowing and doing are in bondage to a will turned in upon itself. When we have developed and refined our awareness and knowledge, when we have come to apprehend and comprehend each other's cultural meanings with great sophistication, we yet may persist in a conflict of vital interests and in our negation of each other's plans for dominating or reorganizing part or all of the world. Greater sensitivity and more comprehensive knowledge are necessary, but they do not resolve the fundamental question of what to do with what we sense and what we know.

A *third* reason is Novak's failure to see the ambiguity in his usage of the term "sensitivity." Sensitivity, for him, is a virtue which, when improved upon and related to action, always yields beneficial results. However, the sensitivity which makes us politically more effective is not identical with the sensitivity which makes us more compassionate and humane. Sensitivity in practical politics makes us more alert to the range and complexity of factors which influence the success of the policy process. In this context, one is sensitive to the cultural and human effects of policies because those effects relate pragmatically to the prospects for success. Depending on the prime determinant of the goals and criteria of policy, a state may be unjust and inhumane while executing a policy informed by keen political sensitivity. On the other hand, if sensitivity is taken to mean deep concern and compassion for persons who are or may be affected by our actions, we may find it necessary to reject on moral grounds certain policies which in terms of practical politics are eminently wise and certain of success. Novak tends to assume that a policy process improved in its effectiveness for achieving political goals will also be more compassionate and humane—and vice versa. He does not distinguish between the pragmatic and the moral meanings of sensitivity, for in a harmonistic view such as his the differences are unreal. Hence he is not prepared to recognize and to cope with the implications of the differences when they appear in political existence.

III.

We need to look also at what Michael Novak is saying or implying about moral theory. He is critical of certain models of moral decision-making, particularly those which he attributes to the "realists." The category "story" provides the basis for a new orientation to moral decision.

Novak's case for the story could have taken as a text the following statement by R. W. Hepburn:

> Most recent British moral philosophy has been dominated by the "rule-obedience" model: moral judgment as the endorsing of principles, commitment to universalizable policies. There have been lately, however, some reminders that, whether or not rule-obedience may be the most satisfactory analysis of moral language, very different models are quite often held by morally sensitive people—by those, for in-

> stance, who see moral endeavor as the realizing of a pattern of life or the following out of a pilgrimage.[9]

Hepburn's essay and the accompanying one by Iris Murdoch show—mainly through the analysis of autobiographical materials—that the nature of the moral life can be characterized and interpreted by means of aesthetic categories such as fable, story and artistic vision and imagination. They contend, moreover, that the aesthetic models give a better account of the elements and data of moral existence than the rule-obedience model. However, they discuss primarily in the dimension of metamorals, and not of morals *per se*. They do not argue that the formal aesthetic models tell us what we ought to do morally, or that they are morally preferable to other models. Novak, however, is interested mainly in a morally improved foreign policy. Also, he believes that an approach to decision-making oriented by the category "story" is morally better than ". . . moral judgment as the endorsing of principles, commitment to universalizable policies." Therefore, we need to try to find out what he believes to be the moral significance of the category.

Does the category itself embody morally authoritative claims? Not if I understand it rightly. Particular stories, of course, generate moral claims, but the category is merely an analytical device. The one possible argument to the contrary is that if the moral life is dramatic by nature, it would impose the formal rule that "we ought to act out (or in accordance

[9] "Vision and Choice in Morality," in *Christian Ethics and Contemporary Philosophy*, ed. Ian T. Ramsey (New York, 1966), p. 181. See also H. Richard Niebuhr, "Metaphors and Morals," in *The Responsible Self*, pp. 149-60.

with) our own story." That would be comparable to the argument of some hedonists that because man (according to their observations) by nature always acts to gain pleasure and avoid pain, he ought to do so. That argument usually is refuted by pointing out that if the pleasure-pain principle describes a biological or psychological necessity, it is pointless to make it a guide to moral action, and that if it makes sense as a moral principle, it implies that man can make choices with reference to criteria other than pleasure and pain. So far as a story-rooted *"ought"* is concerned, someone acts in accordance with his own story because of the immediate authority of the story itself and not because of the authority of a principle which tells him to do so. When he comes to the point of asking whether he ought to act in accordance with the story, he reveals in the asking that the story is not sovereign and that he is responding to claims which transcend it.

However, as I argued earlier, Novak does not seem to be advocating this principle. It is clear, certainly, that he does not want the United States to conduct its foreign policy according to the "American story" he has described. He does argue for a more comprehensive, i.e., a storied, reading of the national interest, and that may imply that we ought to act according to our national interest, properly interpreted with the category "story." But such a reading would create the operational content of national interest by selecting among the many competing stories and interests in the national reservoir. It would not simply uncover the "real" national interest. In fact, the major mystery of this paper is the lack of disclosure of the fundamental values, concepts, or criteria which ought to command the fore and aft of the foreign policy process. The "story" category is not developed adequately for that relationship.

As best I can make out, the category operates mainly as an instrument of the really dominant moral concept in this paper, which is the rule "Always be sensitive to the concrete reality of other peoples." The rule is not formulated thusly, but the formulation certainly is faithful to the ethos and intent of the paper. In view of Novak's very comprehensive definition of "principle," it would count as a principle, also. Despite the strictures against universals, the principle operates as a universal both in the form stated and in the most specific form: "When intervening in the affairs of other people, always be sensitive to their concrete reality and especially to their 'story.' "

But a principle, according to Novak, is supposed to express a story. From what story does that principle come? Not from the "American story" and "sense of reality," certainly, for they predispose to insensitivity. Presumably, then, it comes from some story that the author has not yet disclosed to us, but which influences profoundly the whole argument of the paper. If that is the case, insistence on the principle "be sensitive" amounts to a demand that the United States in its conduct of foreign policy (and therefore in the whole of its national life), as well as others thusly addressed, accept the underlying story which the author is recommending. The root of the issue, therefore, is a call to conversion to a new confessional stance—which implies the affirmation of a more inclusive community of political loyalty, identification and support.

There is, however, another possible explanation for the

principle "be sensitive." It begins with the insistence that sensitivity to the concrete reality of other peoples, and especially to their stories, is prudentially necessary to the effective conduct of foreign policy, whatever its goals and intentions may be. Granted that necessity, the further argument is that the prudential practice of sensitivity requires a degree of openness which corrects the pictures we have of other peoples and statesmen, and challenges our self-image when we see ourselves in the stories and accounts of others. Moreover, the constant improvement in sensitivity for prudential purposes makes us sensitive human beings and not merely sensitive political practitioners. The personal and national transformation which results from the use of the method precipitates—or is accompanied by—fundamental changes in policy. But changes to what, and for what reasons? A theory of virtue according to which the constant and habitual practice of a virtue makes the person or group virtuous does not disclose the basis and aims of a foreign policy. Nor does it fare very well against the Augustinian and Protestant contention that true virtue is possible only within a true relationship of faith, and that the constant and effective practice of what is called a virtue simply makes man more adept in the service of that to which he adheres until called into a new relationship.

I am not sure that I should charge Michael Novak with the foregoing "theory of virtue," for it is not acknowledged and developed as such in his paper. But if that is not his argument for the sensitivity principle, he should provide us with a fuller account of how "sensitivity" is related to "story," and that means, I take it, to *his* story.

IV.

Across the years there have been numerous attempts to come to grips with the implications for politics and morality of cultural and historical relativism. One thinks, for example, of the celebrated lectures of Ernst Troeltsch, written at the end of his life and delivered posthumously at the universities of London and Oxford.[10] Michael Novak's paper on the category "story" is one of those attempts—successful in some ways, but less successful than it might have been because it does not fully engage the basic problem. What kind of moral existence—and what kind of morally responsible foreign policy—can we have once we have recognized the relativity of the very foundations of judgment and commitment?

Certainly the implications for foreign policy of cultural and historical relativism are too vast to be explored in the conclusion to my response to Michael Novak's paper. At best I can point to some of the basic issues and to some of the principal options for working them out in political practice. The first issue is the negation of all efforts to impose truth with material force. Awareness of the relativity of all stories brings every messianic foreign policy under criticism. A cynical imperialism based on self-aggrandizement is not nearly so threatening and so objectionable as one that intends to enforce a particular vision of a just and righteous world order. In this respect, the messianic elements in the American "story" are far more problematical than those which look for the factual and calculable in order to deal "realistically" with political

[10] *Christian Thought: Its History and Application,* ed. Baron von Hügel (New York, 1957).

situations. The latter without the former will serve often as a limiting factor, that is, they will direct the national interests away from situations where the cost-benefit calculations have negative implications. The former with or without the latter predispose the policy process towards over-extension and highly questionable involvements, and with the latter they arrange calculations to support the mission.

On the other hand, over-sensitivity to the idolatrous uses of national power can result in serious failures of responsibility. It may result in a paralysis of the will to use and to use prudently that power which already is present and operational in international politics. It may result in the hesitancy or failure to provide other peoples with aid which in justice and sometimes mercy they ought to have. It may result in the effort to withdraw to the false security of isolation from world conflicts. As the "realists" often have pointed out, the messianic "plunge" and isolationist withdrawal are the alternating tendencies to which United States foreign policy has been predisposed by American experience and American cultural attitudes. The arguments and attitudes attendant on the effort of the United States to extricate itself from Vietnam suggest that the predispositions have not altogether lost their power.

The ultimate issue posed by awareness of the relativity of our views of reality and our stories is whether it is possible to address authentic moral claims to power in a world from which the gods have fled. Are not all things permitted where truth-claims must be prefaced by the word, "It seems to me. . ."? Are not the only realities the power to take and the power to prevent? Perhaps the issue has been overstated. Professor H. Richard Niebuhr used to say that relativism means that we have "views of the universal" but not "universal views." Relativism affirms that all truth claims are particular and relative, but it is not authorized to say that there is no Truth. Nevertheless, so long as we are able to say no more than that it is "our view," we are not justified in requiring anyone other than ourselves to adhere to the moral requirements of that view. Moreover, once we accept that limitation and the reasoning behind it, we are certain to ask why the moral claims should be laid upon us if they are not to be binding upon others.

Several major options are available for dealing with the problems posed to foreign policy by relativism. One is to attribute distortions to transient features of the historical process rather than to man as historical, and to claim a special *gnosis* of the reality and direction of history. The best modern example of this type of gnosticism is Marxism, which charges the biases to the system of property relations, claims a "scientific" knowledge of the dialectical movement of history, and places the engines of "revolutionary power" behind the struggle to realize the classless future. It is a messianic movement determined to enforce its own vision as the truth. From other perspectives, it is demonic and idolatrous. To its own satisfaction, however, it has found the way to transcend the usual limits to the knowing of the truth. It knows the truth, and therefore must cooperate with the historical process in bringing it to full realization.

A second option is frankly to accept tribal identity and to act out the tribal story despite the recognition of its particularity and relativity. We lay hold of our story because that is what we are. We act it out because we can do no other and yet be ourselves. Foreign policy may be placid or it may be buccaneering—depending on the character of the tribal story. The most virulent and destructive historical expressions of this option were the foreign policies of Germany and Italy as fascist states.

A third option is to look to the needs and wants of the self in a world that is judged to have no meaning and therefore no moral guidance or limitation. The ordering of action may be one of unrestrained egoism in which the policy-makers seek to gain for themselves and their society whatever they can. Or it may be one of trying simply to arrange the conditions of survival. Either alternative requires attention to the national story or stories—if they have not lost their cultural power altogether. The first alternative must manipulate the story to support the egoistic policy, and disguise the policy if it conflicts with the story. The second must revise the national story if the story is so aggressive or so timid as to threaten the prospects for survival. However, if the national story has lost its power to command loyalty and to direct action, the prospects are either that a new story will be fashioned in the vacuum or that the society will lose the will to survive.

A fourth option is to grasp plurality and relativity as the grounds and limits of a new story that is being created as it is acted out in the formation of an inclusive international community. The misunderstandings which confuse and misguide the foreign policies of nations can be overcome better by forging historic relationships with commonly understood principles and goals than by increasing sensitivity unilaterally. Roles which formalize and signal constant and typical patterns of expectations exert vastly more moral authority over our behavior when recognized in a story which is ours and in a community to which we belong, than when recognized—however sensitively—in someone else's communal story. But certain limits to the proposal must be made clear. The story cannot be written all at once and then acted out, any more than the inclusive community can be formed in a moment by a common act of will. The story itself is always in process, just as the community at any given moment is a stage of becoming but never a full achievement. The story cannot be written by any one component of international society, but must be the product of the interaction and dialogue of all of them. That means no state or class or race or culture ought to attempt or be permitted to impose its dramatic vision unilaterally on the rest. The new story and new community are discontinuous with the old in that they acknowledge the relativity of the old and attempt to transcend particularity without enforcing uniformity. They are, nonetheless, continuous with the old by reason of moving in process from the elements and forces of the experienced present, and by reason of taking up into themselves the historic particularities as the humanly real.

Foreign policy must serve the national interest as a trust of office. It engages the process of creating the new historic matrix when it executes its trust in such manner as to evoke and strengthen those international relationships which can with authority support and limit the uses of power in the several states.